NEW THINKING AND DEVELOPMENTS IN INTERNATIONAL POLITICS: OPPORTUNITIES AND DANGERS

Edited by
Neal Riemer

Series Editor
Kenneth W. Thompson

VOLUME III
IN THE MILLER CENTER SERIES ON
A WORLD IN CHANGE

Lanham • New York • London

Library of Congress Cataloging-in-Publication Data

New thinking and developments in international politics :
opportunities and dangers / edited by Neal Riemer.
p. cm. — (Miller Center series on a world in change ; v. 3)
1. World politics—1989-
I. Riemer, Neal, 1922- . II. Series.
D860.N4 1991
327' .09' 048—dc20 91-16958 CIP

ISBN 0-8191-8308-3 (cloth, alk. paper)
ISBN 0-8191-8309-1 (pbk., alk. paper)

The paper used in this publication meets the minimum requirements of
American National Standard for Information Sciences—Permanence
of Paper for Printed Library Materials, ANSI Z39.48–1984.

To Robert G. Smith and Julius Mastro

Magnificent Teachers

&

Constant Friends of International Studies

at Drew University

NEW THINKING AND DEVELOPMENTS IN INTERNATIONAL POLITICS: OPPORTUNITIES AND DANGERS

Neal Riemer
Department of Political Science, Drew University

Robert M. Rodes
Department of Political Science, Drew University

William B. Messmer
Department of Political Science, Drew University

Richard S. Rhone
Department of Political Science, Drew University

Douglas W. Simon
Department of Political Science, Drew University

Vivian A. Bull
Department of Economics, Drew University

Donald L. Chatfield
The Planning Center, Tuscon, Arizona

Table of Contents

Introduction

NEAL RIEMER

In this book we seek to explore this provocative question: What has been, and will be, the impact of new thinking and developments upon international politics? We are particularly interested in identifying the opportunities and dangers that we face in international politics as a result of such new thinking and developments—much of it quite amazing to political scientists schooled in the Cold War. We will be particularly sensitive to the possibility of creative breakthroughs in international politics.

The thesis that illuminates the answer to our guiding question—and that knits together the chapters in this book—is as follows: New thinking and developments hold open the possibility of: (1) the end of the Cold War in East-West relations, and the advent of a peaceful, prosperous, and whole Europe in close association with the United States; (2) an invigorated United Nations; (3) a shift of attention to the challenges posed by new patterns of violence in areas of the world—such as the Middle East and the Third World—divorced from the Cold War; and (4) the prospect of global democratization and greater global economic and ecological health.

Will these possibilities fully materialize? Will the last decade of the 20th century see some astounding creative breakthroughs in international politics? Clearly, it is as yet too early to predict affirmative answers with great confidence. The outbreak of war in the Persian Gulf in early 1991 cautions against an easy optimism.

However, it is not too early to begin to assess critically opportunities and dangers. This is a challenging, but imperative, task.

As we enter the last decade of the 20th century—only a few short years away from the auspicious millennial year 2000!—we cannot help but remember those opening words in Charles Dickens's memorable novel, *A Tale of Two Cities*, a novel about the French Revolution. That revolution ushered in the momentous decade of the 1790s, significantly changed the geography and politics of Old World Europe, and had important repercussions in the New World of America and beyond. Wrote Dickens: "It was the best of times; it was the worst of times." Today, we would probably want to edit Dickens's language and say: "The decade of the 1990s *could be* the best of times, *if* opportunities are creatively seized; this decade *could be* the worst of times, *if* theoretical dangers become real, or real dangers become severe." Clearly, it behooves us to seek to understand the new thinking and the new developments which pose both opportunities and dangers, and which challenge us to foster creative breakthroughs in international politics.

In this book we seek to explore new thinking and new developments—as they impinge upon international politics—in several crucial areas. Initially, we will focus on the promise of, or the peril inherent in, a "New Europe" in the making, a Europe that is the arena of the most exciting and promising changes in international politics. Robert Rodes will, in chapter one, highlight Mikhail Gorbachev's understanding of new thinking and the momentous impact of such thinking on the Soviet Union, Eastern Europe, and international politics. It is appropriate to start with Gorbachev's role because in a very significant sense his thought and practice have opened up the possibilities for significant change, not only in Eastern Europe but in Western Europe, in East-West relations, at the United Nations, and indeed in other arenas of international politics. It should be clear, however, that in his new thinking Gorbachev has borrowed generously from Western sources. Moreover, if the phrase "new thinking" is associated with Gorbachev, the impulse to think freshly and creatively about key international problems is abroad and encourages developments throughout the world. William Messmer, in chapter two, illustrates such fresh and creative thinking as he explores new directions for NATO and the problem of European security in the 1990s. He will focus on the future of NATO's role in the context of altered East-West relations, and analyze alternative security patterns for Western Europe. Similarly, Richard Rhone in chapter three will explore new thinking and developments at the United Nations made possible by the ending of the Cold War and the new climate of international politics. The prospects for a new and invigorated United Nations are dramatically being put to a crucial test as a consequence of Iraq's invasion of Kuwait in 1990, the U.N. Security Council's stand against this invasion, and the commencement of hostilities by the American-led coalition to secure compliance with U.N. resolutions. As Cold War conflicts recede it will be important, as Douglas Simon emphasizes in chapter four, to highlight the increasing salience of other patterns of violence. These patterns involve, for example, aggression that threatens to escalate into a regional conflict with severe global repercussions; a host of civil wars; ethnic disputes within nations that seek self-rule; anti-drug wars; political terrorism. These patterns of violence are made easier by the accessibility of weapons of all kinds. Simon's analysis stimulates us to think about more effective ways of dealing with such violence in the post–Cold War world. Moreover, new patterns of international economics, as Vivian Bull will argue in chapter five, are having—and will have—an increasingly important impact upon international politics. Managed creatively these new patterns hold out hope for remarkable economic integration in Europe, for freer trade, and for greater global prosperity. Finally, in chapter six, we stress the importance of the new thinking and developments associated with what we might appropriately call the "information revolution." This revolution—rooted in the modern technology embodied in satellites, radio, television, telephones, xerox and fax machines, computers, and other instruments of rapid communication—enhances constitutional democratization by making it difficult to conceal the brutality, ugliness, and degradation of war, political oppression, poverty, and ecological disasters.

Thus we can more fully appreciate that the influence of new thinking and new developments, and of fresh ideas and creative developments in international politics, cannot be limited to Gorbachev's ideas and practices; or to Western European or U.S.

responses to the end of the Cold War; or to new possibilities that have opened up for the United Nations; or to an appreciation of the salience in the changed climate of East-West relations of acts of aggression and new patterns of violence unrelated to the Cold War. A fuller understanding of international politics requires us also to take into account the growing importance of the impact of international economics and of the information revolution on global politics.

New thinking and developments, it should be clear, pose both opportunities and dangers. The authors of this book will be exploring these opportunities and dangers as they involve the possibility of the best of times or the worst of times in the decade of the 1990s.

The new thinking has been most forcefully called to our attention by the amazing developments that have occurred, and continue to occur, in the Soviet Union and in Eastern Europe, and that—for many—hold out great hope: (1) hope for the end of the Cold War; (2) hope for the lifting of the threat of nuclear war; (3) hope for the emergence of a communism with a human face in the Soviet Union; (4) hope for the peaceful, constitutional, and democratic transformation of once communist regimes in Poland, East Germany, Czechoslovakia, Hungary, Romania, and Bulgaria; (5) hope for successful German reunification.

These amazing developments encourage us to believe that creative breakthroughs in international politics are not only possible, or probable, but may be actually occurring before our eyes. They also challenge us to reexamine other arenas of international politics and to ask about the possibility of creative breakthroughs there—in the whole of Europe; at the United Nations; in other areas of the world such as the Middle East.

CREATIVE BREAKTHROUGHS IN INTERNATIONAL POLITICS

A creative breakthrough in international politics is a successful resolution of a deeply troubling problem. It is a resolution of a problem that the conventional wisdom thinks is impossible. It is a resolution that advances the cause of peace, freedom, prosperity.

In the emerging "new Europe"—for example—we can identify several interrelated problems: involving East-West relations, involving the Soviet Union, and involving the communist regimes of Eastern Europe.

A primary problem in East-West relations is not hard to discern, although it may be phrased in several different ways: Can we really bring the Cold War to an end? Can we really banish the danger of nuclear war? Here we seek to ascertain the impact on international politics of affirmative answers to these questions.

A second problem relating to the Soviet Union can be phrased as follows: Can a powerful communist regime, such as the Soviet Union, really reform itself? That is to say, can the Soviet Union overcome the legacy of Lenin and Stalin, achieve a more authentic democratic and constitutional society, and make a socialist economy work efficiently to achieve abundance and the real satisfaction of authentic human needs? And what will be the impact of reform in the Soviet Union on international politics?

A third problem, involving formerly communist regimes in Eastern Europe, is this: Can these formerly communist nations of Eastern Europe achieve a peaceful transformation to democratic, constitutional, and prosperous regimes? And what will be the significance of such transformations in Europe and globally?

The conventional "wisdom"—we must note—has been negative on all these questions!

The conventional "wisdom" has held that these problems could not be solved. The conventional wisdom affirmed that the Cold War would go on and on—given the ideological, geopolitical, and military antagonisms of "evil empires"—and presumably would not cease until one side or the other was totally destroyed! The conventional "wisdom" also affirmed—and still affirms—the wisdom of nuclear deterrence.

The conventional wisdom (at least in the West) has also affirmed that a democratic, constitutional, and economically prosperous communist Soviet Union is an oxymoron—a contradiction in terms! A communist state cannot be truly democratic or constitutional! And a communist operated economy—a centrally controlled economy—cannot be either efficient, prosperous, or democratic!

Finally, the conventional wisdom has affirmed that communist regimes, once in power, would never give up power freely in a genuinely democratic election. Communist regimes would never allow themselves to be voted out of office! Moreover, the conventional "wisdom" is skeptical of the easy possibility of transformation to democracy, constitutionalism, and prosperity.

It is perhaps too early to say with certitude whether the conventional "wisdom" is entirely wrong, whether a full-fledged creative breakthrough is in the making right now. Nonetheless, Robert Rode's keen analysis in chapter one of Gorbachev's new thinking and its significant impact should lay the foundation for an informed assessment of the possibility of such a creative breakthrough. His presentation sets the stage for a thoughtful analysis of how new thinking bears upon key challenges that we have faced in international politics—challenges that involve both threats to peace, freedom, and prosperity, and efforts to overcome these threats. These challenges in Europe are clear and present.

First, can the key parties involved—both key leaders and the astonishing publics that have emerged—seize the opportunity afforded by significant changes in the Soviet Union and Eastern Europe to put behind us the specter of nuclear war, and of conventional war, between East and West?

Second, can key forces seize the opportunity to encourage genuine liberalization—political, economic, and social—within the Soviet Union and other hitherto communist-dominated governments in Eastern Europe?

Third, can these things be done while simultaneously using the emergence of the new European Community in Western Europe to enlarge both security and prosperity in all of Europe?

What responses does new thinking call for? What are the creative breakthroughs that may be required? Here are some suggested responses with regard to our highly strategic European example. The reader is invited to respond critically to them.

A first response calls for significant East-West nuclear, and conventional, disarmament. (Astonishingly, this already seems to be underway!)

A second response calls for a new East-West security arrangement that would require (1) the reduction and pullback of Soviet forces in Eastern Europe; (2) the reduction and strategic rearrangement of NATO forces in Western Europe; and (3) the unification of the two Germanies, with appropriate safeguards for Germany's neighbors, and within a broader scheme of functional cooperation between Western and Eastern Europe (These developments, it would seem, are also underway! Germany was in fact united in 1990!)

A third response calls for the emergence of patterns of constitutional democracy in the Soviet Union and in Eastern Europe, based—one would hope—on genuinely free elections, a multiparty system, and the protection of human rights. (Here, too, there is considerable evidence of progress toward these goals, although the Soviet Union's repressive reaction to the bid for independence of Lithuania, Latvia, and Estonia clouds the horizon.)

A fourth response calls for the emergence of economic patterns capable of satisfying human needs more effectively, preferably within the framework of freer East-West trade, and of a European Community embracing all of Europe. (Here, although certain economic changes already underway support a move in this direction, significant economic reform and prosperity may take considerable time.)

As we assess these responses in Europe, we need to ask hard questions about new thinking and its possibilities. Particularly we need to ask whether these responses are based on naive, utopian hopes, or on prudent, hardheaded, realistic probabilities rooted both in actual present policies and clearly anticipated developments.

To throw additional light on the challenges facing Europe, and the cogency of suggested responses, and especially of the role of the Western European nations in responding to new thinking, William Messmer will perceptively explore the crucial topic "Remodeling NATO and Europe: Continuity and Change in European Security in the 1990s." The reader is invited to assess critically other suggested creative breakthroughs in international politics as he or she investigates with the other authors of this book new thinking and developments at the United Nations, in the Middle East and the Third World, in international economics, and in connection with the information revolution. We will return to these challenges—and to the theme of creative breakthroughs in international politics—in our conclusion.

THE BEST OF TIMES OR THE WORST OF TIMES?

Opportunities in international politics highlight the possibility of the best of times:

1. The end of the Cold War and of the threat of nuclear holocaust.

2. The advent of a peaceful and prosperous Europe.

3. An invigorated United Nations.

4. A creative and effective response to other patterns of violence in the Middle East and the Third World.

5. A new and prosperous international economic order, responsive especially to nations in the Third World that have been left behind.

6. A significant movement toward worldwide constitutional democracy and ecological health, with significant help from the information revolution.

The dangers in international politics highlight the possibility of the worst of times:

1. The failure of Gorbachev's policy of new thinking (and its promise of freedom and prosperity), the return of conservative hard-liners to power, the resumption of the Cold War, and the prospect again of nuclear holocaust.

2. The failure of democratization in Eastern Europe; and the advent there of political instability, potential chaos, and bloody conflicts.

3. A paralyzed and impotent United Nations.

4. Devastating regional warfare, and the continuation of catastrophic civil wars, ethnic violence, international terrorism, and the deadly drug traffic.

5. The failure to move toward a more equitable world economic order.

6. Set backs for democratization all over the globe.

As we have already suggested, creative responses in Europe-prompted by new thinking and new developments—encourage us to wonder if the 1990s will be the best of times; and not only in Europe and with regard to East-West relations, but also in the Middle East and throughout the globe.

We have already, in Europe, seen some evidence of the best of times—astounding, amazing evidence that few of us would have believed just a few short years ago: (1) greater openness and freedom (relatively, but significantly!) in the Soviet Union; (2) the end of the Brezhnev Doctrine—namely, the insistence on the part of the Soviet Union that once a country had become communist it would stay communist; (3) the fall of rigid, authoritarian communist regimes in Eastern Europe; (4) non-communist groups sharing or achieving power in free elections in communist regimes; (5) a Solidarity leader as president of Poland; (6) a dissident (and formerly jailed) writer as president of Czechoslovakia; (7) the dismantling of the Berlin Wall and the reunification of Germany; (8) official Soviet admission that the Soviet invasion and occupation of Afghanistan and the Warsaw Pact invasion of Czechoslovakia to crush the Prague Spring were mistakes; (9) significant progress on nuclear arms and conventional arms reduction; (10) the possibility of the end of the Soviet Communist party's monopoly of power; (11) moves toward a market economy in the Soviet Union.

But we must not be premature in our celebration of creative breakthroughs in Eastern Europe and in East-West relations! Recent events in the Soviet Union causes observers to question the operational reality, let alone the triumph, of Gorbachev's policies of perestroika and glasnost. Moreover, as we are reminded by the war in the Persian Gulf, and as Doug Simon emphatically points out in his sobering analysis in chapter four, "Violent Conflict in the International System of the 1990s," we need to appreciate new patterns of violence that influence the conduct of international politics. These patterns are particularly apparent in the developing countries in the Middle East, Africa, Asia, and Latin America; but they are also patterns significantly affecting countries in the democratic and communist worlds. Clearly, the decade of the 1990s could be the worst of times *if* (1) centripetal forces in the Soviet Union weaken Gorbachev, produce a bloody right-wing backlash, and thereby result in a relapse into neo–Stalinism; (2) the breakup of the Warsaw Pact and the weakening of NATO undermine the balance of power and the security arrangements in Europe and lead to East-West conflict, or to military conflict between Warsaw Pact countries; (3) a reunified Greater Reich seeks German lands (East Prussia, Silesia, etc.) annexed by Poland after World War II; (4) the weakening of NATO leads to a weakening of the European Economic and Political Community and a loss of the stability and prosperity that has characterized Western Europe since shortly after World War II; (5) the Soviet Union or the nations of Eastern Europe are not able to restructure their political, economic, and social systems to achieve freedom with prosperity, and lapse into conditions of dangerous malaise incompatible with constitutional democracy; (6) Iraq's invasion of Kuwait results in a long, destructive, disruptive war that produces not collective security or a new world order but continuing instability and festering hatred.

Chapters one and two by Professors Rodes and Messmer will throw more expert light on these scenarios of what could be the worst of times in Europe. If there are dangers as well as hopeful opportunities to be seen on the European continent, the outlook in the Middle East and in most of the Third World is grim: *more dangers, fewer opportunities*! Professor Simon, in chapter four, will speak more authoritatively about the larger prospects for global chaos or global order. Our optimism about bright prospects in the 1990s must be tempered by our realistic recognition of dreadful strife around the world, highlighted by the casualties and devastation of the war in the Persian Gulf. Other recent examples underscore the dangers—and the worst of times—in the Middle East and in many countries of the Third World: civil wars in Lebanon, Liberia, Somalia, Ethiopia, Cambodia (Kampuchea); ethnic unrest in the Soviet Union and Yugoslavia; the intifada in the West Bank and Gaza; the struggle against apartheid and black versus black violence in South Africa; the massacre in Tiananmen Square, and repression, in China.

Faced with these examples—and others—we have reason to see the worst of times! We cannot ignore the fact that violence, human rights violations, and poverty are endemic in much of the Third World. Douglas Simon's analysis in chapter four of the varieties of violence in the international system will call attention to a number of disturbing problems and highlight the worst of times. The new varieties of violence to which he directs our attention challenge our capacity for new thinking in a post–Cold War world.

And what of the United Nations? How have new thinking and new developments affected its prospects and its operation? Does the United Nations face the best of times or the worst of times in the 1990s? Most of us are now aware of the historic weaknesses of the United Nations. We are conscious of its limited ability to advance the noble objections of the charter set forth so hopefully in San Francisco in 1945—the admirable goals of peace, freedom, and prosperity throughout the globe. But are we—grown cynical about a United Nations shaped initially by antifascism, then by anticommunism, and then by the anticolonial revolution—missing some significant forces and developments influencing the larger international system? Most notably have we failed to appreciate the impact on the United Nations of the end of the Cold War, and of the forces of complex political and economic interdependence? Given a changed international climate, can the United Nations enhance functional organizations and international "regimes" (characterized by helpful principles, norms, rules, and decision-making processes) that will themselves enhance peace, freedom, and prosperity? In chapter three Professor Rhone's analysis will address these questions and suggest a significantly enhanced role for the United Nations in international politics. He will especially highlight the U.N.'s crucial actions in the Iraq-Kuwait crisis of 1990.

Yet another crucial force in shaping international politics in the 1990s is international economics. Developments here too could make either for the best or the worst of times. In chapter five Vivian Bull highlights the impact of key developments in international economics upon international politics, and upon scenarios of the best of times or the worst of times. Economic integration in Europe, freer global trade, and globalization of business hold out hope for prosperity and peace. But other trends—debt in developing nations, population growth, sticky agricultural issues—suggest real dangers.

In chapter six another key factor also relevant to the best or the worst of times is addressed: the information revolution. Developments here, as we suggested earlier, militate against secrecy, expose oppression, reveal poverty, and open eyes to the possibilities of more prosperous and commodious living. The communication of this information makes it increasingly difficult to sustain tyrannical regimes, to tolerate starvation, to ignore legitimate human needs. The information revolution has enhanced new thinking—understood as openness and reform in the interest of the rule of law, democracy, constitutionalism, effective governance, a vision of a free and prosperous life. The information revolution has also linked up with the ecological movement, a movement which highlights a concern about the need to protect the environment, to balance population and resources, and to guard precious resources. This growing concern is becoming a potent factor in international politics, and the information revolution enhances its global impact. Donald Chatfield, in chapter six, will address these aspects of new thinking in international politics.

Finally, in the conclusion, we will attempt a summary of new thinking and new developments in international politics, and a critical appraisal of the shape of international politics as we approach the year 2000. We will focus, critically, on the prospects of creative breakthroughs in international politics as a consequence of new thinking and developments.

CHAPTER ONE

Implications of Soviet New Thinking For International Politics: Clues From Eastern Europe

ROBERT M. RODES

INTRODUCTION

This chapter will focus on what could prove to be a critical variable in the global political patterns of this new decade, the Soviet Union's relationship with its former satellites in Eastern Europe. Given the extraordinary changes that are sweeping the area, it is hard for anyone asked to think about the region's future not to give way to feelings of helplessness. An analyst is shooting not simply at a moving target but at a multitude of targets, no one of which is necessarily following a fixed trajectory. The analogy comes to mind of the computer-game player who as defender is beset by an ever increasing number of attackers as the difficulty of the game progresses. It is not clear at what point the defense will be overwhelmed, but that it will be is certain.

Our record in predicting the recent past will serve as the point of departure for this attempt to anticipate the future. Specifically, what was being said on the eve of the East European revolution of 1989 regarding the likely direction developments there would take? Most, if not all, observers missed in their calls. One close student of the area reflecting the dominant view of the time concluded:

> Although Gorbachev has raised expectations among Western analysts for dramatic change in Soviet foreign and domestic policy, there is little if anything that he has done or said to suggest that if confronted with a crisis of either kind [either popular revolts in Eastern Europe or attempts by leaders to assert an unacceptable degree of national autonomy], he would behave fundamentally differently from his predecessors. The outlook, then, is for continued Soviet control but no resolution of those underlying dilemmas that made this control difficult, expensive, and a recurrent source of international tension. (Oudenaren, p. 128)

The Soviet Union, in other words, would act true to form; it would maintain control in the end whatever the cost. Why was this opinion dominant, and what led observers to predictions that in the end proved to be so far out of line with what actually happened?

The central argument of this chapter will be that Western failures to predict Soviet actions in 1989 are in good part the result of underestimating the influence on the Soviet world view of what the Gorbachev forces in the Soviet Union have called "new thinking." It will be further contended that understanding Soviet attitudes and actions towards the pivotal events of 1989 provides the best basis currently available for anticipating Soviet behavior in the 1990s. In this estimation 1989 was a moment of truth for Soviet new thinking. The crisis in Eastern Europe that year presented Moscow with the stark alternatives of either reasserting control by force or losing control. Wrapped up in those alternatives was an inescapable choice between new and old thinking. That the decision went in favor of new thinking on such fundamental issues of state is highly significant. An important threshold appears to have been crossed—one consolidating new thinking as the dominant orientation in Soviet foreign policy.

It is necessary to anticipate an objection at this point. One might counterargue that the outcome for the Soviet Union in Eastern Europe in 1989 was determined simply by Moscow's being overwhelmed by events—the same argument essentially that critics have made against *Time* magazine's naming Gorbachev Man of the Decade. Robert Keohane's observation on the quandary of international relations analysis seems appropriate here. "Prospectively, we are unable to predict events; retrospectively, they appear overdetermined" (Keohane, p. 17). Admittedly, Soviet leaders were primarily responding to a rapid and confusing flow of events. Their responses, however, were conditioned in important ways by new thinking. Furthermore, as the argument in the body of this chapter will show, the Soviets did influence the direction events were to take at some critical junctures. A corollary to the argument, then, is that a set of non-new thinkers in Moscow in 1989 might well have arrived at different decisions with fateful consequences.

The line of argument that follows will first direct attention to the question of why Western observers failed to anticipate Soviet responses in 1989. The explanation offered centers on the perception of Soviet interests in Eastern Europe that had become entrenched in Western thinking over the years. Attention will then turn to the body of ideas encompassed by Soviet new thinking. From there the argument proceeds to a consideration of how new thinking may have led the Soviets to redefine their interests in Eastern Europe. The concluding portion of the paper draws on the preceding sections in attempting to anticipate the directions Soviet policy may take in the remainder of this decade.

WESTERN PERCEPTIONS OF THE SOVIET STAKE IN EASTERN EUROPE

Western expectations regarding Soviet policy toward Eastern Europe have been shaped by widely shared views on what Soviet interests in the area have been. These interests have come to be seen as multiple in nature, interconnected, and in a fundamental sense essentially fixed or continuous. Moscow has been commonly assumed to regard at least some of them as absolutely vital interests. Hence their maintenance has been an overriding Soviet concern.

Security has commonly been seen as the core of Soviet interests in Eastern Europe. The territories of today's Poland and

Czechoslovakia have served as the historic invasion routes from West to East. The Soviet experience since 1917 has witnessed two such attempts, each inflicting enormous loss of life and property. Nor were Soviet relations with the independent states of Eastern Europe in the 1920s and 1930s very satisfactory. Poland's attack on a weak Soviet Russia in 1920 and Czechoslovak support for the Whites in the Russian civil war are parts of the unhappy record (Dawisha, pp. 18–19).

Stalin's view of Eastern Europe as a defensive glacis paid for with millions of Soviet lives became well known in the course of the diplomacy of the Second World War. Less understood at the time was the fact that Stalin's notion had its origins much earlier. As far back as 1923 he had argued that Soviet Russia would never be secure without a "ring of brother states" (Rice, p. 661). His position appears to be rooted in his world view, which assumed the inevitability sooner or later of general war between the socialist and capitalist camps. There is every reason to believe he projected the threat forward after 1945 and in so doing retained the notion of Eastern Europe as a vital buffer against an American-led NATO.

Although Stalin's successors may have abandoned many features of Stalinism, they were not seen as differing with him regarding the importance of Eastern Europe to Soviet security. Brezhnev's words to the Czechoslovak Politburo following the Soviet invasion of 1968 are frequently cited as evidence of this continuity in the Soviet outlook.

> Brezhnev spoke at length about the sacrifices of the Soviet Union in the Second World War: . . . At such a cost, the Soviet Union had gained security, and the guarantee of that security was the postwar division of Europe. . . . "For us," Brezhnev went on, "the results of the Second World War are inviolable, and we will defend them even at the cost of risking a new war." And then he said in so many words that they would have undertaken military intervention in Czechoslovakia even if such a risk had existed. (Zdenek Mlynar, *Night Frost in Prague: The End of Humane Socialism*, pp. 239–41, quoted in Dawisha, p. 7)

Nor did the Soviet security interest derive solely from the territory. The armies of Moscow's Warsaw Pact allies accounted for almost half of the pact's forces in Eastern Europe. Though their political loyalties might have been suspect in some cases, the attention and resources devoted to them suggest they were viewed as a far from negligible asset (Campbell, p. 12).

There also appeared to be another side to the security coin. The positioning of a large army in east-central Europe gave the Soviet Union an offensive capacity relative to Western Europe. There is no evidence to indicate Moscow ever seriously intended to exercise this option. Merely possessing it, however, enormously increased the weight of the U.S.S.R. in European affairs (Campbell, p. 11).

Another set of interests fits into a category that could be called political-ideological. Claims to the universality and irreversibility of Marxism-Leninism as a political-ideological system could be validated by reference to Eastern Europe. Campbell argues that Moscow saw having a sizable number of other European states in the socialist camp as vital to its status as a superpower (Campbell, p. 13). Both Dawisha and Campbell seem to agree that Eastern Europe may be vital to the legitimacy of the Soviet system itself. "The collapse of Soviet-style socialism [in Eastern Europe] would have the most serious implications for the legitimacy of communist rule in the Soviet Union itself . . ." (Dawisha, p. 21). Campbell is slightly less categorical but comes very close to the same conclusion on the basis of Soviet action in Czechoslovakia in 1968: "Retreat would represent a failure of huge proportions, an unacceptable loss of prestige, and perhaps a threat to the Soviet regime in its home country" (Campbell, p. 14).

Still another twist on the political-ideological theme has to do with the role of Eastern Europe in the relationship between the Soviet Union and the West. Ideologically conservative Soviets have valued Eastern Europe as an ideological buffer between Moscow and the West, screening out undesirable Western influences. Dawisha sees this attitude reinforced culturally by the Slavophile tradition that has historically influenced a part of the Russian intelligentsia (Dawisha, pp. 9, 20). On the other side are those who see Eastern Europe as a source for innovative ideas and experiments which if successful might be borrowed by the Soviet Union. They, too, have reinforcement from a Russian cultural tradition—that of the Westerner (Dawisha, p. 20).

A third kind of Soviet interest in Eastern Europe is economic. Western analysts have tended to be equivocal on the question of whether economic ties were viewed as vital interests in Moscow. Dawisha observes that it "would be difficult to find many other historical examples of imperial 'centers' that are more impoverished than their 'colonies' . . ." (Dawisha, p. 87). She does not believe that the desire for economic advantage has ever been the primary motivation for the establishment or maintenance of Soviet control.

Economists are mixed in their judgments on whether Eastern Europe has been an economic asset or liability to the U.S.S.R. Stalin did extract resources from the area immediately after World War II through reparations and other means. According to one estimate the total involved was approximately $14 billion—roughly the equivalent of U.S. aid to Western Europe at the time through the Marshall Plan (Dawisha, p. 88). That kind of exploitation tapered off rapidly after Stalin. A number of economists hold the view that in recent years the Soviet Union has subsidized Eastern Europe substantially. This is said to be true especially for the decade of 1971–1980. A Rand Corporation study of those years found that the Soviet Union was spending approximately 2 percent of its GNP in this way (Dawisha, p. 88). Campbell concludes that on "balance, Eastern Europe has been a drain on Soviet resources, although the size of the burden seems impossible to measure" (Campbell, p. 15).

Still another linkage between the Soviet Union and Eastern Europe that has been recognized concerns their prospects for political and economic reform. Charles Gati observed in 1987 that reform in these two parts of the Communist world had proved to be interdependent in a negative way (Gati, 1987, p. 958). A pattern had emerged in which an attempted reform in the Soviet Union would be picked up in Eastern Europe but carried to extremes that would provoke Moscow's intervention, leading in turn to conservatives in the Soviet Union rallying and cutting off or at least curbing reform at home. Khrushchev's program in the middle of the 1950s of de-Stalinization touched off efforts at reform in Hungary and Poland that produced crises in 1956. The alarm felt in Moscow not only led to Soviet military intervention in Hungary but also strengthened the hand of the anti–Khrushchev forces in Soviet politics. Similarly, in the mid-1960s when economic reforms were attempted in the Soviet Union under the auspices of then Premier Kosygin, the reform spirit caught on in Czechoslovakia with results similar to those of 1956—Soviet military intervention in Czechoslovakia in 1968 and the effective abandoning of the Kosygin reforms in the Soviet Union.

The image, then, in the West of the Soviet stake in Eastern Europe that emerges from this review is one of vital interests. It led to conservative estimates as to the likelihood of Moscow tolerating fundamental change in the area even though it recognized that the repeated crises and various troubles afflicting the area were a growing embarrassment to the Soviet Union (Campbell, pp. 13–14). Gati's conclusions in 1987 on the prospects for Gorbachev's policy toward Eastern Europe reflect this point of view.

> What can Gorbachev tolerate in his backyard then? To the extent such distinctions can be made, Moscow's economic needs and especially ideological preferences argue for a more cohesive alliance, while its foreign policy goals point to the benefits of a more autonomous Eastern Europe. Under the circumstances, Gorbachev can allow for far less autonomy than his allies need; and hence they, in turn, can aid his domestic priorities and facilitate his policy of detente far less than he wants them to. He cannot begin to end the cold war by transforming Eastern Europe from a Soviet sphere of control and domination into a Soviet sphere of influence. He cannot permit Eastern Europe to combine membership in Soviet-led military and economic alliances with internal and even considerable external independence—the way another Eastern European country, Greece, has come to relate to the West. (Gati, 1987, p. 74)

Western assessments of Soviet interests in Eastern Europe seemed to lead to an inevitable conclusion regarding the future of Soviet foreign policy: the Brezhnev Doctrine remained operational for Moscow. Formulated in 1968 as the rationale for the Soviet suppression of the Prague Spring, the doctrine proclaimed the right and responsibility of the members of the Socialist community of states to intervene in the internal affairs of a fellow member if socialism was in jeopardy. Gorbachev, however inclined he might be to tolerate diversity in Eastern Europe, would act in the spirit of the Brezhnev Doctrine if events went beyond a certain point.

NEW THINKING: REVISING THE SOVIET WORLD VIEW

It is time now to turn to a broader context—to the new thinking on international relations that had begun to emerge in Moscow—as a preliminary step to considering how these ideas were to affect the Soviet-East European relationship. It is important to note at the outset that new thinking was not the result of a purely abstract intellectual process. Its endorsement and formulation into a programmatic statement was first of all a political act. New thinking was devised to support a particular political agenda—Gorbachev's agenda (Lynch, pp. 3–4). That is not to say that the ideas themselves are not believed; it is merely to argue that they are especially attractive because they appear to justify a particular course of political action and set of priorities.

Gorbachev's role in the emergence of new thinking is interesting. Many of the ideas it incorporated had been formulated before he took office in 1985. They were circulating among specialists within the policy "think tanks" of the Soviet Academy of Sciences even in the days of Brezhnev. Gorbachev himself does not appear to be a major author of the new outlook. After all, he is, as his adviser Fyodor Burlatsky told the Kennan Institute, "a political figure, not a philosopher—first he goes to the river, and then he tries to find a way to cross" (Kennan Institute, 5 December 1989).

Nevertheless, he is the first top Soviet leader since Lenin to hold a university degree. Perhaps because of that he appears much more open to new ideas and diverse opinions than his predecessors. He greatly expanded the circle of advisers to the Kremlin. He and his immediate colleagues saw themselves as modern in outlook. It is hard to resist the conclusion that Foreign Minister Shevardnadze was not projecting the Soviet leadership's self-image when responding to a reporter's question about his impression of the new Romanian leaders who replaced Ceausescu.

> The Romanian leaders left a most favorable impression—they are erudite, modern people with analytical minds. The contrast to Ceausescu and his "team" is striking. There is an entirely different intellectual potential and cultural and educational level. (*Izvestiya*, 8 January 1990, condensed in *The Current Digest of the Soviet Press*, 7 February 1990, pp. 22–23)

Interested in the new ideas in part for the justification they could provide for his course as political leader and in part for the guidance they could offer along that course, Gorbachev's contribution has been primarily one of endorsement and advocacy.

The key to Gorbachev's course as political leader appears to be that he has believed all along that commitment to internal reform has to be the overriding priority for the Soviet Union even if his notions on the content of that reform were not necessarily clear or complete. Two competing images have developed of him as a reformer. One holds that he came into office with relatively modest intentions. Under pressure from events and learning on the job, he has moved progressively toward more and more far-reaching change.

Another way of looking at the man is to see his seemingly hesitant beginning down the path of reform as really a tactic allowing him to consolidate his power before alarming the inevitable conservative opposition prematurely. Following the party congress in early 1986 which offered him the opportunity to introduce major changes of personnel in the leading party bodies, he became noticeably more outspoken about the scope of needed reform. The verbal progression from moderate reformer to radical reformer is easily traced in his public utterances. He avoided even using the word "reform" for a year or so after becoming leader. Yet in his book on perestroika published in 1987, he referred to his reform program as "revolutionary in character" and a "sequel" to the 1917 Revolution—strong words in a country where 1917 has been habitually treated as the ultimate revolution resting on a pedestal by itself (Gorbachev, p. 50).

Regardless of which interpretation is correct, it should be clear by now that in the context of the Soviet Union of the mid-1980s Gorbachev has become a radical reformer or, perhaps more accurately, transformer. He has not only completed Khrushchev's work of demolishing Stalin's reputation. By the decisions he led the Central Committee to adopt at its meeting in February 1990 he has also cleared the way for jettisoning important parts of Leninist (the vanguard party) and Marxist doctrine (public monopoly of ownership of the means of production) in practice if not in name.

From this perspective it is possible to see the adoption of new thinking more clearly as a political act. Given his commitment to reform as a priority, he was attracted to a view of the world which portrayed an international environment that would not only permit Soviet concentration on internal reform but might aid the process as well.

Three themes of new thinking appear to be especially relevant to our concerns: the primacy of domestic policy over foreign policy, the idea of common security, and the concept of the common European home. Gorbachev has argued that the primacy of domestic policy over foreign policy is a necessity for a Soviet Union seeking to carry out far-reaching domestic reform. In a nationally televised speech to an international forum on peace and disarmament in Moscow in February 1987, he combined a statement of the priority of Soviet domestic policy over foreign policy with a plea for a world order which would support such an arrangement.

> Before my people, before you and before the world, I state with full responsibility that our international policy is more than ever determined by domestic policy, by our interest in concentrating on constructive endeavors to improve our country.
>
> That is why we need lasting peace, predictability and constructiveness in international relations. (*New York Times*, 17 February 1987)

Though it might have been appropriate at the time to approach these words with caution, it appears in light of subsequent action that they were an accurate reflection of his orientation.

The concept "common security" is not of Soviet origin. Its original development was in the report of the Independent Commission on Disarmament and Security Issues which was published in 1982 under the title of *Common Security* (Dawisha, p. 210). Cyrus Vance, who was one of the commissioners, notes that the report

> received a mixed reception at first. But when the new Soviet leader, Mikhail Gorbachev, espoused the need for "new thinking" on both domestic and foreign policies in 1985, a breakthrough occurred. Having studied the Palme Commission report, Mr. Gorbachev embraced both the concept of "common security" and many of the commission's proposals. (*New York Times*, 27 May 1989).

The full significance of Gorbachev's endorsement of common security only becomes apparent when it is viewed in the context of traditional Soviet thinking on national security. In his memoirs Henry Kissinger summed up his understanding of the outlook of Russia's rulers both under the czars and the Soviets by observing that they identify

> security not only with distance but also with domination. They have never believed that they could build a moral consensus among the peoples. Absolute security for Russia has meant infinite insecurity for all its neighbors. (Quoted in Legvold, pp. 99–100)

Certainly that interpretation is appropriate for Stalin, who seems to have held to the end to the view that war between the Two Camps was inevitable in the long run. His successors abandoned parts of Stalin's outlook when Khrushchev denied the ideological thesis of war's inevitability in 1956. In doing so he cleared the way for improved relations with the West in the form of detente. Jack Snyder notes, however, that Khrushchev's view of detente—one which Brezhnev would share—might properly be called "offensive detente" (Snyder, p. 103). War with the West was not inevitable in the nuclear age, but what was keeping the imperialists at bay was a powerful Soviet offensive capability. It would be hard to devise a better rationale for a continuing Soviet military buildup.

By adopting and popularizing the concept of common security Gorbachev was now arguing that unilateral security for one nation at the expense of another is no longer possible (Gorbachev, p. 142). Equal security is the only real security. He also pointed to the way that over-arming could be self-defeating for the Soviet Union; in what was an unprecedented acknowledgement from a Soviet leader he conceded the reasonableness of other countries seeing a potential threat in "the very fact of the U.S.S.R.'s immense military might" (Gorbachev, p. 202).

Common security served Gorbachev as a basis for calling for change in a number of specific areas of security policy. He downgraded the military component in defense by arguing that in today's world security had to be achieved primarily through political rather than military means. He provided a rationale for military reductions by insisting that "reasonable sufficiency," not superiority, should be the criterion for force levels. He argued that military forces should be reorganized so as to conform to a strategy of non-offensive defense; it would mean cutting back on those armaments such as tanks, which gave a capacity for surprise or quick attack. In so doing he was striking at the strategic orientation of the offensive which for decades had guided the Warsaw Pact and defined its requirements for military forces.

A complementary development proceeding apace in Moscow was the redefining of the external threat which Soviet leaders had always insisted their country faced. An article published in early 1988 in the party's theoretical journal appears to have been the start of the public phase of this campaign. The authors directly challenged the orthodox ideological position on the aggressive nature of Western imperialism. They maintained that the combination of existential nuclear deterrence and democratic traditions rooted in Western societies effectively curbed imperialist tendencies. The West was not interested in aggressive war "or any other war for that matter" (Lynch, p. 49).

The third element in new thinking of special relevance to our concerns is the theme of the common European home. Gorbachev introduced the idea in 1985 and has employed it with increasing frequency and emphasis since 1987 (Malcolm, p. 664). The concept is related to the general notion in new thinking of an increasingly interdependent world but stresses the special ties of Europe as a region and an idea. Some observers see as the primary motivation behind the Soviet interest in the concept the desire to bring Western Europe into greater economic involvement with Eastern Europe (Stent, p. 3). Moscow is looking ahead to the Europe of 1992 and does not want to be left out. In 1988 the Soviets ended their long-standing policy of nonrecognition of the European Community when CMEA (Council for Mutual Economic Assistance) entered into an agreement with the EC, opening the way for agreements between the EC and individual members of CMEA (Stent, p. 5).

The common European home concept, however, is broader than economics or Europe in the geographic sense. Its scope extends officially from Vladivostok to Vancouver following Gorbachev's signing a joint statement in June 1989 with West German leaders that recognized the United States and Canada as legitimate members (Malcolm, p. 667). It is intended to have political-security dimensions as well as economic. Gorbachev made that point clearly in his address that July to the Council of Europe.

> I do not claim today that I have a ready-made blueprint for such a "home." Instead I shall speak of what, in my view, is the main point—namely, the need for a restructuring of the international order in Europe to bring to the fore all European values and make it possible to replace the traditional balance of forces by a balance of interests. (Gorbachev, 7 July 1989, p. 4)

EASTERN EUROPE IN THE LIGHT OF NEW THINKING

The crucial question as the East European Revolution of 1989 approached was whether the Soviet leaders would be guided by their new thinking or by the reflexes toward Eastern Europe that had been acquired in the more than 40 years of Soviet tutelage. It was not an easy question to answer in advance. Taken literally, the new thinking would seem to give a meaning to Eastern Europe for the Soviet

Union that is radically different from the one it had held traditionally. For one thing, new thinking seemed to reduce the significance of Eastern Europe in important ways. What remained, for instance, of the notion that Eastern Europe as a defensive glacis was a vital security interest of the Soviet Union? By reducing, if not eliminating, the idea of a militarily aggressive West, new thinking seemed to deprive the Warsaw Pact of an enemy. With its stress upon political rather than military approaches to security, it seemed to downgrade the value of the Warsaw Pact forces. And by endorsing a strategy of nonoffensive defense it seemed to deny the utility of Eastern Europe as a springboard from which pressure could be placed upon Western Europe.

Seen in the light of new thinking, the desirable role for Eastern Europe might be more that of a bridge than a buffer. The road to the common European home would require cooperation with Western Europe and the United States. Bringing them into the area to assist the hard pressed East European economies would be more important than keeping them out. Soviet behavior in the area would be crucial to building confidence in Moscow in the West.

But there were strong grounds for doubts. The extent to which the new thinking was genuinely believed was unclear. It might be little more than a clever exercise at public relations. Even if it were believed in whole or part, would it be acted on in a crisis?

There were certainly signs that the Soviets were at least beginning to think about the heretofore unthinkable. One indicator was the holding in July 1988 of an unprecedented conference of Soviet and American specialists on Eastern Europe. The subject for discussion was "The Place and Role of Eastern Europe in the Relaxation of Tensions between the U.S.A. and the U.S.S.R." It appeared to be a significant step away from the traditional Soviet position that treated Eastern Europe as their exclusive zone. The Soviet delegation spoke with candor about the serious problems of the area and placed some of the blame on Soviet policies. It was agreed to hold a second conference the following year ("East-West Relations and Eastern Europe," p. 55).

As the East European situation grew increasingly unstable in 1988, attention began to focus on the question of whether or not Moscow continued to adhere to the Brezhnev Doctrine. A number of statements by Soviet figures seemed to indicate the doctrine had been repudiated. Academician Oleg Bogomolov, director of the Soviet Academy of Science's Institute of Economics of the World Socialist System, was reported to have told the Soviet-American conference on Eastern Europe that

> The Brezhnev Doctrine is completely unacceptable and unthinkable. . . . We gave too much advice before to our partners, and it was actually very damaging to them. It's time to keep our advice to ourselves. ("East-West Relations and Eastern Europe," pp. 55–56)

The previous February he declared on Hungarian television that "the internal structure and foreign orientation of Hungary could evolve into something like those of Austria and Sweden" without being seen as a threat in Moscow (Svec, p. 50). Gorbachev himself in his speech to the Council of Europe in July 1989 appeared to repudiate the Brezhnev Doctrine when he said the "philosophy of the 'common European home' concept rules out the probability of an armed clash and the very possibility of the use of force or the threat of force—alliance against alliance, inside the alliances, wherever" (Gorbachev, 7 July 1989, p. 5). On his trip to Finland in October he declared that Moscow had no right to interfere in the affairs of the East European countries (*New York Times*, 27 October 1989). It was also known that East European leaders were increasingly doubtful that Moscow would intervene to rescue them if they lost control (Gati, 1989, pp. 102–103). Nevertheless, the suspicions of some were aroused by the failure of Gorbachev to condemn past interventions (Gati, p. 102).

Along with the declaratory statements there were at least a couple of Soviet actions that bore directly on the issue. By signing the European agreement of 1986 on confidence-building measures the Soviet Union had seriously reduced its ability to intervene militarily through surprise attack in Eastern Europe. Under the terms of that agreement a member was to give advance notification of exercises involving more than 13,000 troops and permit outside observers. Unless it violated the agreement, Moscow could not have mounted the kind of operation it employed in 1968 in

Czechoslovakia. Likewise, Gorbachev's announcement in December 1988 of his plan to withdraw 50,000 Soviet troops unilaterally from Eastern Europe was seen in the area as an indication he was not contemplating military intervention (Kramer, p. 61).

The question of whether the principles of new thinking would be honored was not answered conclusively until the Polish governmental crisis in July 1989. By urging the Polish Communists to enter a Solidarity-dominated coalition government Gorbachev signaled conclusively Soviet acceptance of a non–Communist outcome. The pattern was repeated in October when Moscow apparently let the East German government know that it could not count on support from Soviet troops in East Germany should it crack down on demonstrators and find itself in trouble (Flora Lewis, *New York Times*, 12 November 1989). Though these Soviet decisions could not have been predicted with certainty, in retrospect the trail of statements and actions pointing to them looks unmistakable.

THE 1990s

Throughout the first year of the new decade Soviet foreign policy in many ways appeared to proceed in line with the new directions that had emerged in the 1980s. Though in one sense these events might be seen as logical followups to this new orientation, that should not blind us to their stunning novelty and momentous importance. The previous year had ended with the fall of the Berlin Wall but with the issue of German reunification unresolved. At the outset of 1990 who would have predicted that by July Moscow would have indicated its willingness to accept not only German reunification but also the new Germany's remaining in NATO? The schedule for dissolving the remaining Soviet military presence on German territory was fixed in September when East and West Germany and the Four Powers with rights in Germany stemming from the postwar occupation period signed, in Moscow, the Final Settlement with Respect to Germany. All Soviet troops were to be removed from the Eastern part of the country by 1994. Further undercutting of the military dimension of the once imposing Warsaw Pact occurred when Moscow reached agreements with the new governments in

Czechoslovakia and Hungary under which Soviet troops are to be completely withdrawn from those countries by July 1991.

On the broader European scene, the signing of the Conventional Forces in Europe agreement in November appeared to spell an end to the long feared Soviet offensive capability aimed at the NATO countries. By setting equal limits for East and West in Europe in a series of critical categories of conventional armaments the agreement would not only require the Soviet Union to carry out major reductions but also forfeit quantitative advantages it had long enjoyed. As one surveys the drastic retreat of Soviet power in Europe, it is difficult to think of historical parallels. What other country, short of one suffering defeat in war, has surrendered its international position to a comparable degree?

Nor did the reorientation of Soviet policy stop at Europe. Regional conflicts in the Third World that for years and in some cases decades had provided an arena for competition between East and West were being addressed anew by Moscow and Washington. From Nicaragua, to Southern Africa, Ethiopia, Cambodia, and Afghanistan, progress was made in moving the two outside powers nearer to parallel policies. The United Nations began to experience a rejuvenation, especially in its largely dormant role of maintaining international security. Unprecedented Soviet cooperation enabled the Security Council to authorize military action against Iraq for its aggression in Kuwait—action against a country with which Moscow had been aligned and deeply involved for decades.

Yet the year would close with observers of the Soviet scene in a much more somber mood. Conditions inside the country were widely perceived as deteriorating rapidly. Pictures of stores with empty shelves conveyed the message of an economy tottering near collapse. Growing separatist sentiments among the various nationalities posed the question of how much of the country would remain together and raised the ultimate specter of civil war. The political situation grew increasingly confused. The gulf between President Gorbachev and the democratic movement of reformers to his left widened precipitously. A swing to the right became more and more evident. Apparently Gorbachev had come to fear that the country was lurching toward chaos and concluded that order, not further change, was the need of the hour. He turned to the police and military for help. The relevance of domestic politics to Soviet foreign policy was made unmistakably clear when Eduard Shevardnadze, the foreign minister who had presided over the remarkable turns of recent years in Soviet foreign policy, resigned almost a year to the day from the opening of the Berlin Wall and issued a warning of impending dictatorship.

As part of our effort to anticipate the outlines of Soviet foreign policy in the remainder of the decade it is useful at this point to return to the question posed at the beginning of the chapter. Why did Western attempts to forecast Soviet behavior in the crisis of East European communism prove to be so overly cautious in their estimates of Soviet willingness to accept change? At least three reasons emerge from the discussion pursued thus far: (1) a persistent tendency to underestimate the depth of commitment of the Soviet leaders to domestic reform and the extent to which that carried priority in foreign policy; (2) a comparable tendency to underestimate the degree to which new thinking had altered the Soviet world view; (3) an overestimation of the continuing strength of the Soviet desire to maintain a sphere of domination.

The centrality of internal reform in the outlook of Gorbachev and his allies looms as especially fundamental. Gorbachev's claim quoted earlier to the effect that never before had domestic policy determined foreign policy to such a degree appears to be well founded. The process of reform was real and running deep at the time. Suspicions then voiced in some quarters in the West that perestroika was really *peredyshka*—a tactical breathing space before the Soviets returned to their true selves once again—missed the point. What Gorbachev had been instrumental in unleashing in Soviet society was a profound process of change. He was simultaneously attempting to steer it and being driven by it. The attempts at reform were responses to a compound crisis involving fundamental questions about political authority, economic organization, and the nature of a multinational community. Fyodor Burlatsky, an adviser to Gorbachev, presented a striking forecast of the difficulties ahead and the likely protracted nature of the process of reform in remarks made at a time when the prospects for perestroika seemed considerably brighter than they would by the end of 1990.

> This is only the beginning of a very complex process. *In 20 or 30 years* [emphasis added] the Soviet Union will become a new, open society with a pluralistic economy and political system, and human rights guarantees. It will become part of European Civilization. (Kennan Institute, 5 December 1989)

Given the close links that seem to exist between the new directions in Soviet foreign policy and the process of domestic reform, it is important to examine the prospects for reform in the less promising atmosphere prevailing at present (February 1991). Burlatsky's comments, quoted above, offer valuable perspective. One conclusion that seems warranted on the basis of the experience with reform in the Soviet Union over the past several years is that the road to fundamental change is in all probability going to be long and messy. The swing to the right currently proceeding in the U.S.S.R. is a setback, but it would be premature for supporters of reform to give way totally to despair. For one thing, Gorbachev's intentions and needs at this time are far from clear. It would be a strange outcome indeed for someone who has run the risks he has to bring about change suddenly to become a new Brezhnev. His vision of the Soviet Union's desired future might not be the one favored by liberal democrats but still could be a far cry from the old Soviet status quo. He may be waiting for a more auspicious moment to resume reform.

As for the resurgent right, little is known regarding how strong they really are. The political situation is simply too confused to judge whether or not they have the power to impose their policies on Gorbachev. It is not unreasonable to fear that the Soviet army, smarting from the collapse of the external empire, sees a new mission for itself in maintaining the internal empire. The current friction between the American and Soviet governments over the ratification and implementation of the Conventional Forces in Europe agreement may be an early sign of growing military influence. So too could be the increasing stickiness of the all-but-completed START negotiations. In assessing the prospects for the conservatives, however, it is well to keep in mind the underlying cause of the move toward reform in the 1980s in the first place—the absolute failure of the old system's performance when measured by international standards. Glasnost made the failure all the more obvious. There is little evidence that the right has answers to the long-term systemic problems facing the country. Their prescriptions are likely only to deepen the impasse. Should they continue to discredit themselves by clumsy actions like the attempted crackdowns in Lithuania and Latvia in January 1991, opportunities for reformers may broaden.

Nor should it be forgotten in the present difficult circumstances that the Soviet cup of reform, though partly empty, is also partly full. The country is substantially different from what it was only a few years ago. Real gains were made during the 1980s in expanding freedom of speech and communication, as well as the right to organize and participate meaningfully in public affairs. In the process expectations were raised still higher. Moscow now has to take the republics seriously as the dynamics of Soviet politics have shifted outward from the center. It is by no means clear how manageable the country would prove to be if an attempt were made to restore the old methods of control. An informal system of checks and balances may exist to a degree and prove to be an additional complication for conservatives.

So what conclusions for foreign policy might be drawn from these considerations? If reformers regain the upper hand (as seems quite possible, at least in the longer run), the new directions set by the end of the 1980s would presumably be reinforced. More challenging is the question of what might occur in a period of conservative dominance. Given our image of Soviet hard-liners, it is easy to expect the worst. A little caution, however, might be warranted even here. The new thinking of the 1980s in Soviet foreign policy and the new directions for which it provided a rationale have in fact created a new international reality for the Soviet Union. The retreat of Soviet power from Eastern Europe and the collapse of the communist myth that accompanied it mean that a return to a conflictual and competitive approach in foreign policy would only leave the Soviet Union more isolated in the world than ever as it struggled with internal problems that stood little chance of being resolved without substantial outside assistance. More probably perhaps than a radical turn would be a loss of coherence in foreign policy as the country became more divided and preoccupied with its internal problems.

BIBLIOGRAPHY

Campbell, John C. "Soviet Policy in Eastern Europe: An Overview." In *Soviet Policy in Eastern Europe*, edited by Sarah M. Terry. New Haven: Yale University Press, 1984.

Dawisha, Karen. *Eastern Europe, Gorbachev and Reform: The Great Challenge.* New York: Cambridge, 1988.

"East-West Relations and Eastern Europe (An American-Soviet Dialogue)." *Problems of Communism*, May-August 1988, pp. 55-70.

Gati, Charles. "Gorbachev and Eastern Europe," *Foreign Affairs*, Summer 1987, pp. 958–975.

________. "Eastern Europe on Its Own." *America and the World 1988/89 (Foreign Affairs)*, pp. 99–119.

Gorbachev, Mikhail. "Gorbachev's Address to the Council of Europe." *News and Views from the USSR*, 7 July 1989, pp. 1-14.

________. *Perestroika: New Thinking for Our Country and the World.* New York: Harper & Row, 1987.

Hough, Jerry F. "Gorbachev's Politics." *Foreign Affairs*, Winter 1989/90, pp. 26–41.

Kennan Institute. *Meeting Report.* 5 December 1989.

Keohane, Robert O. "Teaching How to Ask Questions about International Relations." *News for Teachers of Political Science*, Spring 1989, pp. 17–19.

Kramer, Mark. "Beyond the Brezhnev Doctrine: A New Era in Soviet-East European Relations?" *International Security*, Winter 1989/90, pp. 25–67.

Legvold, Robert. "War, Weapons, and Soviet Foreign Policy." In *Gorbachev's Russia and American Foreign Policy*, edited by Seweryn Bialer and Michael Mandelbaum. Boulder: Westview, 1988.

Lynch, Allen. *Gorbachev's International Outlook: Intellectual Origins and Political Consequences*. Boulder: Westview, 1989.

Malcolm, Neil. "The 'Common European Home' and Soviet European Policy." *International Affairs*, Spring 1989, pp. 659-676.

Meyer, Steven M. "The Sources and Prospects of Gorbachev's New Political Thinking on Security." *International Security*, Fall 1988, pp. 124–163.

Oudenaren, John Van. "The Soviet Union and Eastern Europe: New Prospects and Old Dilemmas." In *Central and Eastern Europe: The Opening Curtain?*, edited by William E. Griffith. Boulder: Westview, 1989.

Rice, Condoleeza. "The Making of Soviet Strategy." In *Makers of Modern Strategy: From Machiavelli to the Nuclear Age*, edited by Peter Paret. Princeton: Princeton, 1986.

Snyder, Jack. "The Gorbachev Revolution: A Waning of Soviet Expansionism?" *International Security*, Winter 1987/88, pp. 93-131.

Stent, Angela. "The Soviet Union and Western Europe: Divided Continent or Common House?" *The Harriman Institute Forum*, September 1989.

Svec, Milan. "East European Divides." *Foreign Policy*, Winter 1989-90, pp. 41-63.

CHAPTER TWO

Remodeling NATO and Europe:
Continuity and Change in
European Security in the 1990s

WILLIAM B. MESSMER

Stunning events have occurred in Europe since 1989 and they have substantially influenced discussion and policy on European security. The fall of the Berlin Wall in late 1989 was followed within months by the beginning of the process of withdrawal of Soviet troops from most of Eastern Europe, and the emergence of new democratically elected governments in place of old dictatorships. By the summer of 1990, East Europe's security organization, the Warsaw Pact, had ceased to function as a military pact. There were also significant changes elsewhere in Europe in response to East Europe's shift. In conjunction with Soviet withdrawals, the United States also began to reduce its military strength in Western Europe. By October 1990, Germany was fully united and symbolized Europe's overcoming of its former Cold War division. Subsequently, in November 1991, a conventional forces treaty that substantially reduced armaments of East and West was signed at a Paris summit of all of Europe's leaders.

In this maelstrom of international events which have transformed the hostile, polarized Europe of Cold War days, some suggested that the North Atlantic Treaty Organization (NATO) should be disbanded as no longer necessary. Others argued that NATO's continued presence was unnecessarily provocative to the

Soviet Union. The 16 member nations of NATO, however, elected to keep the alliance intact at a meeting in London in July 1990. As important as the decision to keep NATO, however, was the accompanying promise to substantially remodel military aspects of the alliance, and to encourage roles for other European organizations in promoting regional trust and confidence across the former boundaries of East and West. Thus, as the final decade of the 20th century got underway in Europe, the member nations of NATO had collectively outlined a security agenda for NATO that promised fundamental continuity as well as significant change.

The central arguments presented here are that, given the continued uncertain outcome of Europe's changes in the aftermath of the Cold War, retaining NATO was surely prudent. Furthermore, because of its encouragement of change, NATO will continue to play a central role in Europe in the post–Cold War period. However, before discussion of NATO's agenda for both its own remodeling as well as its influence on regional security, an analysis of the reasons for the retention of NATO will be useful in understanding more about the fundamental aspects of security in Europe.

SOVIET AND GERMAN THREATS TO PEACE

The decision on the part of the leaders of the alliance to keep NATO was widely supported, despite the demise of the Warsaw Pact, because NATO serves to reassure its members with regard to two specific security concerns: The first is the future character of the Soviet Union, and the second is that of the new, reunited Germany. Both nations are currently following paths and leaders that make them seem unlikely to threaten the peace. However, each has the size and potential capability to threaten the security of their neighbors. More than this potential, however, each has a recent history of actually being a threat, and this makes it difficult for those concerned with European security to entirely ignore this possibility.

NATO is a source of support for those who continue to be concerned about a security threat emanating from the Soviet Union. The potential of a Soviet military threat to Western Europe, of course, is the reason for NATO's existence in the first place. Under

Gorbachev's leadership, the reduction of Soviet forces and the relinquishing of political control in the other members of the Warsaw Pact have considerably reduced the U.S.S.R.'s attack capability. Nonetheless, the Soviet Union remains the largest nation in Europe with a population of 280 million, and it is still a military superpower with nuclear weapons and conventional military forces that dwarf that of any other European nation.

In addition to its military power, retaining NATO was necessary because in this age of glasnost and perestroika, the Soviet political situation is still very fluid. It could change further in virtually any direction. The political culture that has given such great power to Gorbachev to undertake such drastic changes is still present. It has not only put Gorbachev in power, but also Stalin before him. Furthermore, the fundamental nature of the political and economic reforms and the conservative opposition to them, as well as the nationalities problems within the Soviet Union, raise the possibility of instability and even civil war there.

In early 1991 the use of force by local military units against separatists in the Baltic republics led to the loss of civilian life and intensified fears that a return to the repressive ways of the past might be immanent. It is especially noteworthy, in this regard, that the nervousness of both Czechoslovakia and Hungary over Soviet moves in the Baltics have pushed each to announce their probable resignation from the Warsaw Pact by June 1991. Each has also sought to develop a relationship with NATO over security matters.

Thus, there are strong fears about the future government in the Soviet superpower. In the words of one British observer, "Mr. Gorbachev is a charming fellow; perhaps he means well. But who knows what—or who—will come along next." (Davidson) The possibility of a backsliding, insecure, and perhaps unstable Soviet Union, by virtue of its substantial nuclear and conventional military capability, remains a potential threat to the rest of Europe.

Even with the successful development of multiparty pluralism in the U.S.S.R., the rest of Europe may well wish to maintain some coalitional arrangement capable of offsetting Soviet power. Democratic leadership in the U.S.S.R. will be no absolute guarantee that it might not wish to intervene in the rest of Europe to attain political or security ends that it finds desirable. The United States has, despite its democracy, and in some instances because of the pressure on government generated by its democratic nature, seen fit to intervene in the affairs of smaller nations close by and elsewhere to attain security ends that were perceived as significant. It is not yet time for NATO to pass out of existence because of a diminished Soviet threat to European stability.

The second potential security problem felt to be important by many in Europe is that of Germany. Despite its recent history of 40 years of stable, cooperative, democratic government, Germany is a source of anxiety because of its role as aggressor in the two major wars of this century. Germany's growth and gradual rearmament in the post–World War II period have not been undertaken independently. Rather, Germany's military forces, since its entry into NATO in 1955, have always been intertwined in the development of NATO's defenses. Thus, Germany has no real recent history of sovereign national control of its military capability.

The reality of not knowing how Germany might act if it were not in NATO is coupled with the fact that West Germany, by 1990, had the most advanced economy in Europe. It was twice the size of France's economy, and was only smaller than that of the United States and Japan of the world's market economies. This economic base gives modern Germany a tremendous military potential. This potential has been further enhanced by its unification with East Germany, and by the fact that Soviet troops, which remain as part of the reunification settlement, are to be removed by 1995. The combined population of 80 million citizens of the united Germany is approximately 20 million larger than either France or Britain.

A united Germany's membership in NATO enables Germany's Western neighbors to observe directly, through the intertwining of NATO's forces, Germany's enhanced military capability. The unification of Germany would be very difficult for other Europeans to accept without the presence of NATO in which an enlarged and more powerful Germany will be enmeshed. The still present concern about German power is the reason why the other member states of NATO, and even most of those nations of the Warsaw Pact, insist upon Germany's continued membership in NATO as part of the terms of unification. It is also the reason that, as part of the unification process, the Soviet Union has insisted on the right to maintain its own troops in what was East Germany for up to four years after unification.

WAR AMONG NATO'S EUROPEAN MEMBERS

The insistence on maintaining a unified Germany in NATO highlights two additional aspects of the alliance which make it a desirable organization. NATO has enduring value that is different from its capacity to defend its members from outside threat, such as might be posed by the Soviet Union in the future. In the context of Europe's history, the presence of NATO has facilitated the creation of conditions that make war among the West European members of the alliance unlikely. Just as NATO reduces the fear specifically of Germany by enmeshing it in NATO, so, in general, NATO reduces the likelihood of hostility among any of its European members. Foremost among the conditions which encourage this stability are: NATO's formal incorporation of the United States, with its superior military capability, into European security arrangements and, through its consultative, political, and integrated military command, the creation of a regional unity and defense identity among Western European political and military elites. These factors have helped to create an alternative to the troublesome, national approaches to defense of the past.

Diplomatic historians of Europe outline a pattern for the region of considerable instability, national animosity, and warfare that goes back over the centuries (DePorte). At heart, the problems of Europe have sprung from the conflicting interests and visions of the nations and political elites that make up the region. Each nation has a history of competition with other nations, and the resulting suspicions and hatreds have bred strong nationalism in the European context that has been partly defined by its xenophobia.

Accompanying the rise of nationalism has been the development of the pattern of the balancing of power among the nations of the region. Periodically, one nation has arisen within Europe, imbued with its own sense of identity and mission, that has sought to extend its control well beyond its borders, often through military conquest. Historically, Europe created, from among its own nations, a coalition of forces that could offset the power of any one of them. Thus, a rough pattern for the balancing of power among the contending nations emerged. So, in turn, in the 400 years prior to the 20th century, the bids for European hegemony or empire of first Spain, and subsequently Austria, and then France, were successfully defeated by shifting military coalitions of other Europeans. Countless smaller attempts to adjust borders and change Europe's geopolitical realities were also met by opposing coalitions that sought to balance off the power of nations not satisfied with the status quo. Thus, "balance of power" policies often best described the reality of international politics in Europe in recent centuries.

The contributions of NATO to European security must be considered in light of this history. In the 20th century the nationalisms of Europe were further intensified by the all-out struggle of the two world wars. In these instances, however, the inability of purely European coalitions to balance off newly unified German power set up conditions for the entry of the United States into these Europe-centered wars. From the American perspective, U.S. entry into world wars I and II against the Germans was necessary to keep Europe and all of its resources from coming under the control of a political and economic system that might have ultimately projected its hostility toward the United States. Playing this role also required the United States to come to change its own pre–20th century isolationist heritage in world affairs.

This pattern of a U.S. role in European affairs continued after World War II. The Soviet Union, under the leadership of Stalin, emerged from the war with great military power and ideological vision of the future and took actions against its East European neighbors that created the perception that the Soviet Union was a new threat to the rest of Europe. Thus, in 1949, this time to forestall war, the United States returned a third time to play a central role in the emergence of an anti-Soviet coalition. NATO is the embodiment of this coalition.

One of the fundamental characteristics of NATO, therefore, and one that may be overlooked, is that it is a mechanism that does facilitate the ongoing, direct involvement of U.S. troops in the European security balance. The London Declaration, thus, says:

> The significant presence of North American conventional and U.S. nuclear forces in Europe demonstrates the underlying political compact that binds North America's fate to Europe's democracies.

The North Atlantic is a wide natural barrier, and in this century, when balancing Europe has required the presence of the United States, the existence of NATO removes any doubt that might exist in the mind of a potential aggressor about whether the United States has enough of an interest in European security to actually become involved in military action there. The presence of U.S. forces in Europe as part of the NATO's troop deployment has also been a reminder to a more geographically isolated American electorate that it has an ongoing interest in European security. Thus, "Atlanticism," or the link across the Atlantic which includes the United States in European security, is facilitated by NATO.

Transcending the centuries of Europe's mutually hostile nationalisms and their transition into a cooperative, regional identity in areas of defense policy has also been encouraged by the presence of NATO. This process has been eased by the presence of a common Soviet enemy over the decades since World War II. But it has also been facilitated by NATO, because of its political decision making and consultation apparatus and its international secretariat. In this way, NATO has provided a mechanism that has encouraged a unity in security matters that goes beyond individual nations. The supreme decision-making body of the alliance is the NATO Council. On this council sit the permanent, ambassador-level representatives of the 16 member nations. Several times a year, other national governmental representatives, such as the defense ministers and foreign ministers, meet for consultation. Also, periodically, the heads of state of the member governments will meet for direct discussions, as they did in London in July 1990. In addition to the council, there is a NATO Parliament made up of selected members of the elected national legislatures of member nations of NATO. While this body is essentially consultative, it serves the very important function of creating continual face-to-face contacts on security matters among elected civilian politicians of the national systems of Europe. This intricate web of political contacts creates an important domestic political base in the member nations that can be a voice on behalf of transnational unity.

In a similar manner, NATO's integrated military command helps to encourage a perspective that transcends nationalism. In NATO's military structure, the fighting units are taken from the national militaries of the member nations. The military staff which commands and does the planning and creation of overall military strategy for these national units, however, is made up of officers from all the member nations. The supreme allied commander of NATO's continental forces has always been an American, though the rest of the command and staff is made up of military personnel from all member nations. The exceptions to this are France and Spain, who are members of the council, but have decided to make their contributions to NATO outside of the integrated command.

The integrated command has been a mechanism which has fostered a meshing of national military leaderships for a collective purpose. It has created a web of personal contacts and working relationships that have countered the national antagonisms derived from the past. It is in this way that NATO goes beyond the looser and less stable coalitions of Europe's past, and through the integrated command binds Western Europe's national military establishments into a firm alliance.

Nationalism is not a thing of the past by any stretch of the imagination. Far from it; nationalism is still a major force among Europeans.   What NATO has done, however, through its organization, is to create an identity which can counter pure nationalism. Thus, from this perspective, NATO functions as a forum where the political and military elites of historically antagonistic European nations, along with the United States and Canada, may come to be reminded of the benefits of the peace and security which they now share in common.

Living in the capitals of Germany, Britain, and France today, it is absurd to think that they might rain fire and death on each other as they did in living memory. But such cataclysm seems absurd at least partially because of the security cooperation made real in the more than 40 years of NATO's existence. Without NATO, who could guarantee a peaceful version of European events since 1945? NATO does not just "keep the Americans in and the Soviets out"; it also "keeps the Europeans apart," as the old saw goes. NATO's continued existence, in the face of the momentous and potentially destabilizing changes underway in the 1990s, can help to avoid the "renationalizing" of security policy among Western European nations.

These characteristics of NATO that make its presence still desirable for the immediate future, and perhaps longer, do not mean that it should not be adjusted to better fit the present circumstances. The role of NATO is to insure European security. Thus, changing to meet new circumstances so that it may better fulfill its role is clearly an option that had to be taken.

THE CHANGING SECURITY CONTEXT

Just as there are strong reasons for the maintenance of the NATO alliance, there are also compelling reasons for remodeling it. Most fundamental to encouraging this remodeling was the process of change within the East bloc and the desire on the part of the West to encourage it to go further. The other important factor in bringing change to NATO was the change in the West, itself, in which Europe, through the European Community (EC), has been moving successfully toward greater economic and political integration. As a consequence, confidence has grown that European integration, which itself reduces security tensions, could be extended in the future to include the changing Eastern nations. To achieve this greater economic interaction between East and West requires the removal of impediments to normal East-West interaction, such as NATO, which in the past has publicly focused on the East as the enemy.

Eastern Europe is no longer an immediate military threat to Western Europe, and this has been the most important factor in the chain of events leading to NATO's remodeling. The reduction, which began in 1989, of the number of Soviet troops in the other nations of the Warsaw Pact, with the exception of what was East Germany, has been nearly completed by 1991. Further, the Soviet willingness to allow political change toward democracy in the other Warsaw Pact nations was crucial in reducing the sense of threat felt in the West. The Warsaw Pact, itself, met formally in June 1990, to declare itself a diplomatic forum, and no longer a defensive military alliance. As mentioned, two members, Hungary and Czechoslovakia, have indicated that they will withdraw from the Warsaw Pact by June 1991, and seek some relationship with NATO. These momentous changes came on the heels of the Soviet leadership's clear desire to achieve nuclear and conventional arms control agreements and reduction of tensions with the West.

The changes in the East bloc also brought governments that were bent on a transition to economies with free markets and private property. Thus, the governments of the East bloc not only no longer posed a security threat, but in the important political and economic spheres, they sought to emulate the West. Refusing to respond positively to these fundamental changes by the Warsaw Pact nations was no longer politically supportable in the Western democracies. Thus, the stage was set for NATO's remodeling.

The July 1990 NATO communique reflected, in its initial paragraph, the impact on NATO of the new political and economic reality in Eastern Europe:

> Europe has entered a new, promising era. Central and Eastern Europe is liberating itself. The Soviet Union has embarked on the long journey toward a free society. The walls that once confined people and ideas are collapsing. Europeans are determining their own destiny. They are choosing freedom. They are choosing economic liberty. They are choosing peace. They are choosing a Europe whole and free. As a consequence, the Alliance must and will adapt. (London Declaration, Art. 1)

The new security situation in Europe, in which the old East-West balance was dissolved, had a particular impact on the Soviet Union that also could not be ignored by NATO. From the Soviet perspective, it left the U.S.S.R. alone to face NATO, however benign, without its former allies. It also created a situation in which the U.S.S.R., by acquiescing to the reunification of Germany, faced the prospect of little direct influence over an enlarged Germany. This was particularly significant because the Nazi invasion of the Soviet Union during World War II had cost approximately 20 million Russian lives. While the West took satisfaction in Germany's choice of the West, it recognized that this new reality was a source of unease for the U.S.S.R., and a situation that future Soviet leadership might try to alleviate. After all, the U.S.S.R. is still a military superpower and, in the long run, if it is insecure it will create tensions, if not worse, for all of Europe.

As these shifts took place in the security alignment of Europe, President Gorbachev was simultaneously trying to carry out the internal democratization of his country against conservative, orthodox communists and fearful Russian nationalists, who wanted to halt the process of domestic and international change. The insecurity of Russians in the face of German unification within NATO was a theme that the Soviet conservatives and nationalists were using to galvanize support within the U.S.S.R. against Gorbachev.

Gorbachev himself, to provide a vehicle for greater Soviet influence in the evolving new European security order, and to soothe his conservative opposition, called for the dissolution of both NATO and the Warsaw Pact and the creation of a new continent-wide security system in which the U.S.S.R. could play a part. Given the democratic changes underway in the U.S.S.R. itself, many in the West, while reluctant to give up NATO, wanted to provide Gorbachev with support in his efforts at domestic Soviet reform. Changing NATO to a less threatening posture was one way to provide this support. The London Declaration acknowledged this motivation in its remodeling in the following manner:

> We recognize that, in the new Europe, the security of every state is inseparably linked to the security of its neighbors. NATO must become an institution where Europeans, Canadians and Americans work together, not only for the common defense, but to build new partnerships with all the nations of Europe. The Atlantic community must reach out to the countries of the East which were our adversaries in the cold war, and extend to them the hand of friendship. (Art. IV)

The second fundamental change in Europe's security context was the change in Western Europe. The success of the European Community (EC) in fostering economic and political integration among the West European members, along with the security integration within NATO, in turn made war among them seem almost impossible. In the words of one scholar of EC integration,

> The European Community, by developing common interests, policies, laws, and institutions, has become the embodiment of . . . a system of common security. War between its member states is now inconceivable; it is no longer feasible. (Wistrich, ch. 8)

The success of the EC has led to growing confidence that, in the long run, economic integration across all of Europe was now possible. This could alleviate nationalist impulses and security tensions that made the Cold War alliances and the dangerous division of Europe come into existence in the first place.

The motivation to develop economic relations with the East is also based upon the belief that such interaction will bolster East Europe's fledgling democracies. This will further serve to reduce security tensions in the post–Cold War era. The words of Sir Michael Alexander, the U.K.'s current NATO ambassador, best capture the sentiment felt by many:

> Nations which elect governments genuinely accountable to their peoples usually become more stable, predictable places from which the risk of aggression is vastly reduced.

The hope for greater European economic unity is reflected in many ways in Europe's current political dialogue. It is implicit in the phrase, "common European home," made popular by Gorbachev. It is also present in the phrase, "Europe, from the Atlantic to the Urals," associated with de Gaulle's vision of Europe two decades ago, but nonetheless heard frequently today. Also, the often heard phrase of "common security," which defines security as something that requires trust and arms control among nations, or put simply in the London Declaration as ". . . the security of every state is inseparably linked to the security of its neighbors," is an internationalist approach to security that subtly encourages the idea of European unity that transcends East and West.

Confidence that economic unity can be created between East and West is running high in the 1990s. It is interesting to note, however, that if the changes in Eastern Europe had occurred in the mid-1980s, the idea of pursuing a greater European unity that incorporated, somehow, both East and West, would have been much more muted. It was just in 1987 that the widely respected British author John Palmer wrote pessimistically about the potential even of a united Western Europe. In the mid-1980s, many felt that the EC was stagnant with only limited success at overcoming national trade barriers (Palmer). In 1987, changes that streamlined the EC's decision-making process, and then brought the acceptance of the Single European Act (SEA), by which all trade barriers will be removed by 1992, vastly improved the situation (Leonard, ch. 2). The EC has generated considerable momentum toward unity based upon these changes. In doing so, it has captured the interest and imagination of many European politicians, business leaders, and ordinary citizens alike.

A "European" perspective and culture have begun to emerge. The changes, acquisitions, and mergers in the corporate world are indicative of this. As traditionally national European companies have tried to position themselves so that they can best take advantage of the new wider market, they have begun to think "European" rather than primarily in national terms. American- and Japanese-based multinationals have rapidly begun to acquire European corporations so that they may have an opening in Europe's single market. Such firms bring in with them, as outsiders, an already developed European perspective (Fuerbringer). Government ministers of many departments have developed a weekly or monthly routine that involves travel to and consultation with their counterparts in other European governments or with the appropriate commissions at the EC level. The inevitable consequence of this is to begin to think "European." The career plans of university students now routinely include the thought that they will work elsewhere in another European country, as they fit into the widening corporate structure.

It is also of more than passing interest to note, as a result of the increasingly successful EC unity and economic growth associated with it, the major social democratic and socialist parties of the

European Left have altered their traditionally hostile views of the EC as a "capitalist club." The British Labour party has most recently come around to this perspective, and in June 1989 for the first time fought an effective campaign for seats in the EC Parliament. The French Socialists under Mitterrand came around to this perspective in the mid-1980s after their lack of success at purely French national development of socialism. The West German Social Democratic party has also come through a similar transition in the 1980s (Telo). All of these parties have dropped their traditional goals of ultimately nationalized, state operated, noncapitalist economies, and have adopted a stance in which they seek only an efficient and humane management of their capitalist economies as intertwined in Europe as a whole.

In the current circumstances of the development of regional and global corporations, most political parties, and actors, whatever their ideology, have been losing confidence in their national political systems' capacity to control transnational capitalism effectively. They have begun to see the EC as a continent-wide buffer and political management mechanism that will enable them, in partnership with other EC members, to deal with international capitalism. The much discussed Social Charter of the EC, which is supported by most parties because it focuses on the rights of workers and citizens as the single market emerges, while a product of socialist and social democratic concerns and influences, is just one example of where the shift to "Europeanist" thinking on the part of most parties can be seen.

Economic cooperation between East and West cannot occur in depth until free markets and democracy are further entrenched in Eastern Europe. Investments cannot move into the East and be reasonably certain about the political stability of the systems until these conditions are fulfilled. Consequently, a debate has emerged about the pace at which Western nations should seek to aid and encourage such cooperation. However, what is widely agreed upon is that such interaction should take place. It has been said by some that the changes in the East bloc have intensified the drive for economic and political unity within the EC so that it remains stable in the face of Eastern disintegration. But it is also true, given the EC discussions that suggest the possibility of developing formal relations with the East, that the drive for further unity within the EC has come about so that it is in a stronger position to begin to include the Eastern nations at some time in the future (Andriessen).

The lesson of both the EC and NATO is that the right type of regional institutions can bind nations with similar systems and interests together in ways that overcome their potentially destructive national differences. The rewards of cooperation and integration outweigh those of national separation and economic competition. The confidence is present that a broader European unity that spans East and West can be achieved through the EC, and even perhaps, someday, NATO.

The timely, simultaneous occurrence of these two separate events, the change in the East and the growing momentum toward EC unity, have, together, encouraged NATO to remodel militarily as well as pursue a diplomatic agenda that would make the alliance an agent of change toward the normalization of relations between East and West.

MILITARY REMODELING FOR A UNITED EUROPE

NATO's plan for military change has been influenced by the simultaneous needs of remaining militarily secure, but of not being so strong militarily that it threatened the Soviet Union. NATO's military remodeling has had to tread the fine line between these two goals. Moving too far toward one could jeopardize the other. The plan of military adjustments that might achieve these ends was announced at the July 1990 NATO summit in London.

The communiqué of NATO's London summit, or as it is often called, the "London Declaration," promised changes in several important aspects of both the conventional and nuclear armaments and strategy of NATO. These changes sought to provide substantial reassurance to the U.S.S.R., given the virtual end of the Warsaw Pact as a military alliance, that NATO would not threaten it. The member states of NATO, thus, wanted the Soviets to understand that the retention of NATO was a reasonable but not threatening precaution for Europe in its unsettled state at the end of the Cold

War. If this could be achieved, NATO would not be a barrier to further changes.

In order to remodel its military features, NATO first insisted on the achievement of a treaty between the Warsaw Pact (though in reality the Soviet Union) and NATO, which brought parity in conventional arms at much lower levels than had historically existed. In the words of the document:

> To reduce our military requirements, sound arms control agreements are essential. That is why we put the highest priority on completing this year the first treaty to reduce and limit conventional armed forces in Europe. . . . (London Declaration, Art. 12)

In the view of NATO, such a conventional arms treaty was necessary because of the superior amounts of Soviet arms present in Eastern Europe and Russia since the close of World War II. This conventional arms superiority has always been at the heart of the West's view of the Soviets as a threat. The founding of NATO in 1949 was based on the need to defend against this large Soviet military capability that could be readily used to subdue nearby Western Europe.

NATO's London Declaration also announced two additional and planned changes in NATO's conventional force arrangements that were based upon the precondition of a conventional arms reduction treaty. The first was support for a limit on the number of armed forces of Germany after it was united. A limit of 370,000 troops was subsequently promised as part of the "4 + 2" unification talks on Germany that took place between authorities of the four occupying powers of the United States, U.S.S.R., U.K., and France, and representatives of the two Germanies before the October 1991 unification. This, along with Soviet troops remaining in Eastern Germany until 1994, was asked for by the U.S.S.R. as a condition of unification in which Germany remained a member of NATO.

The second conventional change would limit the offensive capability and change the strategy of those conventional forces that would remain after a treaty. Such weapons as tanks—which have unique offensive, as opposed to defensive, capabilities—would be singled out in such arrangements for special limitation. Offensive weapons, such as tanks, allow the rapid projection of national military power, and as such are perceived as a particular threat to stability. In the words of the communique, NATO would,

> . . . work to limit the offensive capability of conventional armed forces in Europe, so as to prevent any nation from maintaining disproportionate military power on the continent. (London Declaration, Art. 13)

Along with the change in arms capability, a change in the alliance's conventional warfighting strategy would also be adopted. NATO has always referred to itself as a defensive alliance that will not attack first. This is a principle that was reaffirmed in the London Declaration. Until changed, however, the conventional strategy of NATO has been referred to as a "forward defense." This means that NATO will station most troops close to the potential battle line, and it will seek to project any fighting forward onto the territory of an aggressor. Thus, it is an "offensive" defense that seeks, once attacked, to quickly blunt the attack and then carry a counterattack onto the enemy base, disrupting rear-area staging and resupply.

This type of defense strategy, adopted in the decades before German unification, was especially appealing to an already geographically undersized West Germany, which did not want a more conventional military defense that was based on giving up territory to allow an attacking enemy to run out of momentum. NATO's "offensive" defense strategy has been specifically titled, "Follow On Forces Attack," or FOFA, for short. FOFA requires the presence of mobile offensive weaponry, which, as indicated above, is viewed as especially threatening and de-stabilizing. Changing this strategy from an offensive to a "defensive defense" is especially important to the Soviet Union, which traditionally viewed it as a way to plan an attack on the Warsaw Pact, under the guise of defending Western territory. Agreeing to the principle of limiting offensive weapons capability, and the change of conventional strategy that is based on such weapons, are especially important in helping to reduce military tension and normalize relations between East and West.

As a part of the decision to seek lower arms levels and a different strategy, NATO has also indicated that it will restructure the remaining units, primarily those found in Germany, so that they are stationed further to the rear and are more mobile so that they may respond with greater speed and versatility. Perhaps of greater interest, however, is the planned extension of the principle of force integration found in NATO's integrated command. In principle, smaller fighting units will remain national in character, but they will be increasingly integrated into larger, multinational corps. The implication of this decision is that, as overall NATO troop strength is reduced in Germany, German troops will nonetheless remain integrated with units from their alliance partners.

Serious negotiations between NATO and the Warsaw Pact to achieve a Conventional Forces in Europe (CFE) Treaty began in Vienna, in 1989. An accord between the United States and the Soviet Union, alone, in February 1990 announced an agreement to reduce the troop levels of each superpower in Europe to approximately 195,000. Encouraged by this, the larger CFE process, which included all members of both alliances, agreed finally on key aspects of the conventional arms situation by the fall of 1990. The actual CFE Treaty was formally signed by the leaders of the nations of both pacts at the Paris meeting of the Conference on Security and Cooperation in Europe (CSCE) in November 1990.

The CFE Treaty was primarily an agreement about military armaments. It included agreements on equal but much lower numbers of tanks, armored vehicles, artillery, helicopters, and aircraft for each pact. Thus parity at lower levels was achieved. There was also an acceptance of the principle that no single country could provide more than two-thirds of either pact's equipment in these categories. This was included so that the Soviet Union might not enlarge its armaments by using the Warsaw Pact levels as justification. The CFE Treaty did not cover total troop levels of both pacts and negotiations were to occur in subsequent meetings in Vienna. However, given the low levels of equipment outlined by the CFE Treaty, and the prior agreement between the United States and the U.S.S.R. on troop strength, this was less important.

The CFE Treaty was a clear acceptance of NATO's conventional disarmament agenda called for in the London

Declaration. It removed the decades old superior Soviet conventional threat, which, as the subsequent nuclear discussion below will make clear, made possible the other changes in NATO's defenses promised by the London Declaration. This, in turn, helped insure that the U.S.S.R. did not perceive NATO as a threat. That this latter point was the case seems clear in light of the Soviet acceptance of the CFE Treaty while NATO continued as an important, and perhaps the only, European security forum left after the Cold War.

In its London Declaration, NATO also offered further fundamental changes in the nuclear armaments of East and West. The proposed changes in nuclear weapons were acceptable to NATO providing that a CFE treaty was signed. This condition having been met, nuclear changes are now underway. Nuclear weapons are traditionally viewed by NATO as being necessarily present in its arsenal as a deterrent to any fighting, and in particular as a deterrent to the large number of Soviet conventional forces. Nuclear weapons are so terrible in their effect on life, and even the potential life of future generations, that many credit them with keeping the peace in Europe during the worst hostility and tension of the Cold War era. Thus, the doctrine of "nuclear deterrence" calls for the presence of nuclear weapons in some form in the West as the ultimate guarantee of peace.

The assumption that nuclear weapons are a deterrent to war has not changed. As the London Declaration reaffirms,

> [Nuclear weapons] will continue to fulfill an essential role in the overall strategy of the Alliance to prevent war by ensuring that there are no circumstances in which nuclear retaliation in response to military action might be discounted. (Art. 18)

Thus, some form of nuclear weaponry will remain in NATO's arsenal. What has changed is a willingness to reduce the number of nuclear weapons, and how they might be used in any conflict.

NATO's current nuclear strategy of "flexible response" combines the use of conventional and nuclear weapons in its response to an attack. Conventional forces would first be used to stop an attack.

If they did not end the threat, then small nuclear weapons, such as nuclear artillery shells, would be used. If these smaller devices would not stem an attack, then ever larger ones would be used, up to and including the largest ballistic missiles that protect the U.S. homeland. It is this nuclear warfighting strategy that will change.

The allies, in signing the London Declaration, promised in the aftermath of a CFE accord to "reduce their reliance on nuclear weapons." To encourage this process, the London Declaration offered the complete removal of all nuclear artillery shells if the U.S.S.R. would do the same. NATO has, therefore, offered to remove the first rung on the nuclear escalation ladder envisioned in the flexible response strategy. While there have been no agreements between the Soviet Union and NATO yet about the removal of tactical nuclear weapons, the Soviet Union has also offered to remove its tactical nuclear weapons. In the aftermath of the CFE Treaty, NATO has promised to introduce a new defensive strategy by May 1991 that will presumably no longer be based upon a low nuclear threshold or a forward defense such as FOFA.

In earlier moves, NATO had already decided to put off the modernization of the short-range Lance missiles stationed in Germany that are also part of the first rung of flexible response. In the 1988 INF Treaty with the U.S.S.R., all ground-launched, intermediate-range missiles were removed from NATO's arsenal. Nuclear weapons, such as free-fall bombs from aircraft, sea-launched missiles, and the remaining Lance missiles, which will not be obsolete until the mid-1990s, remain in both the short and intermediate-range categories of nuclear weapons. However, the offer to remove the artillery shells, most likely to be used first in hostilities, in combination with the earlier decisions has gone a considerable way toward easing the threat of nuclear war that has existed for many years in Europe.

The London Declaration, in the jargon of nuclear arms control, has made it possible to significantly "raise the nuclear threshold" in warfighting scenarios in Europe. Thus, in offering to give up its nuclear artillery shells and change its strategy of flexible response, NATO has not completely abandoned the concept of nuclear deterrence, but it has substantially encouraged the process of making nuclear weapons, as the London Declaration indicates, "truly weapons of last resort" (London Declaration, Art. 18).

NATO'S DIPLOMATIC AGENDA: AN OPENING TO THE EAST

Just as significant as the military changes offered by NATO are the efforts to open a political relationship between NATO and the East. Through its London Declaration, NATO suggested that a regular set of political relationships be established between the alliance and the nations of the Warsaw Pact that would enable formally working out such improved relations. These suggested steps to improve relations are an extremely important part of easing tensions when considered against the hostility and mistrust which have characterized East/West relations in the past.

The first step suggested by NATO to help in the creation of a political relationship between East and West was a direct response to the Warsaw Pact's earlier declaration that NATO was no longer its enemy. NATO's response was the call for the signing among the member nations of the two alliances of

> . . . a joint declaration in which we solemnly state that we are no longer adversaries and reaffirm our intention to refrain from the threat or use of force against the territorial integrity or political independence of any state. . . . (London Declaration, Art. 6)

Subsequently, at the Paris CSCE meeting at which the CFE Treaty was signed, a mutual pledge of nonaggression was signed among the 16 members of NATO and the six remaining members of the Warsaw Pact. The nonaggression agreement contains a principle which appeals to all Europe. It would offer some measure of protection not only for the members of NATO against the U.S.S.R., but for the smaller nations of the Warsaw Pact caught between the Soviet Union and Germany. It is also noteworthy that the pact would be among individual states, and not pact to pact, so that the very act of agreeing to nonaggression would not formalize a role for the military pacts that most symbolize Europe's hostile division.

NATO also took the unprecedented step of inviting the political leaders of the Eastern European countries to speak to NATO. Vaclav Havel, the president of Czechoslovakia, has accepted NATO's offer and is scheduled to address a NATO meeting in March 1991. The London Declaration also endorsed the earlier invitation by the Soviet Union to have NATO's secretary-general, Manfred Wörner, visit Moscow for consultations. Wörner quickly accepted and visited Moscow in July 1990 shortly after the adjourning of the NATO London Conference, to initiate the direct dialogue sought by both sides.

The dialogue among political leaders inaugurated by Wörner's visit to Moscow and Havel's visit to NATO is remarkable. However, in the long run the additional step of inviting political representatives of the Soviet Union, Czechoslovakia, Poland, Hungary, Romania, and Bulgaria to "establish regular diplomatic liaison with NATO," may be more meaningful. This will regularize contact between the alliance and the individual members of the Warsaw Pact. In the words of the London Declaration, "This will make it possible for us to share with them our thinking and deliberations in this historic period of change" (Art. 7). It may also prove significant that the offer was made to the specific nations by name rather than to the Warsaw Pact as a whole. This makes it possible for the move to be more than a confidence-building step. It may also be a preliminary step toward making NATO the base of a new wider European security order, with this as the opening step to ease the transition of former Warsaw Pact members, such as Hungary and Czechoslovakia which have indicated interest, into NATO.

On the level of military staff, the London Declaration also encouraged the establishment of more formal and possibly regular contacts between the top military commanders of the U.S.S.R. and NATO. It also suggested a Europe-wide meeting of all military leaders in order to promote "common understanding" among those military professionals.

The final part of NATO's diplomatic agenda was the endorsement of a more active role for the Conference on Security and Cooperation in Europe (CSCE). The CSCE is a 34-member organization which includes all 16 of the member states of NATO, including the United States, Canada, and Iceland, as well as the six remaining member nations of the Warsaw Pact, and the 12 neutral and unaligned nations of Europe. Albania is the only European nation that is not a part of CSCE, and it has now indicated an interest in being represented. CSCE amounts to a pan-European forum plus the non-European members of NATO.

The CSCE is a product of the Helsinki Conference of 1975 that was to bolster detente between East and West and to provide a place in the process for those European nations outside of the existing blocs as well. One aspect of the accord reached as a result of the Helsinki process focused on legitimating the postwar boundaries in Eastern Europe. For this reason, the East bloc regimes and the U.S.S.R. signed the accord. The Helsinki Accord also encouraged the protection of domestic human rights, however, and it is this legacy that the accord and CSCE are best known for. Within the East bloc, the Helsinki Accord was used by dissidents as a legal basis to urge further internal political changes on their governments since that time. It is credited as helping to lay the moral and legal base for the groups that encouraged the East European democratic revolutions of 1989.

A genuine desire to encourage Europe's greater unity in the 1990s has brought CSCE into focus again as an institutional base for such unity. Its association with the positive changes already taking place in East Europe has given it momentum in this regard. It is also the only regional structure in place whose membership already spans the East-West gap and includes all of the other neutral nations of Europe as well. Furthermore, a wide array of prominent opinion in both East and West, expressed by Mikhail Gorbachev in the East, as well as by former British defense minister, Denis Healey, and U.S. Senator Joe Biden, has suggested that the CSCE should gradually assume the responsibility for Europe's security and ultimately replace NATO and the Warsaw Pact (Biden).

Perhaps in the long run CSCE might play such a role. But several factors work against this occurrence at least during the next decade or so. Given the enormous shifting that is occurring and the potential for political instability that is present in East and Central Europe, this seems premature. The wisdom of asking member states of NATO to abandon the alliance to join another with yesterday's enemy, before years of institutional stability and trust develop in the East, is highly questionable.

The problems of decision making and effective action in CSCE would have to be addressed. CSCE has no military staff or command. In sheer political terms CSCE would have enormous problems as an effective decisionmaker. It is currently so large, with so many different national interests and security traditions, that it may prove unwieldy even if the trust is developed between East and West. The capability of such an organization to respond to a security problem with other than words is questionable. Because of the wide variety of nations and perspectives involved, CSCE might be reduced to impotence because it would presumably be capable of acting only where consensus existed. The examples of the frequently deadlocked U.N. Security Council, or the OAS, come quickly to mind in evaluating CSCE as a replacement for NATO. It is quite possible that prematurely abandoning NATO for the uncertainty of CSCE is to invite the renationalization of the security policy of those members of NATO and might constitute the base for a future arms race among current NATO neighbors.

These weaknesses of the CSCE, combined with NATO's strengths, encouraged the alliance to take another tack on CSCE. The London Declaration encouraged a strengthening of CSCE and its consideration as a pan-European diplomatic forum for the consideration of many political and security-related issues. NATO's endorsement of the CSCE does give Gorbachev and the U.S.S.R. something of what he has called for, because the CSCE provides a forum in which the U.S.S.R. might play a prominent role and thus not be closed out of the formal diplomatic consideration of security issues being explored in the new Europe.

NATO does not intend to invest CSCE with responsibility for security, at least in the short term. The primary indication of this is the fact that the London Declaration suggests several political functions for CSCE but clearly omits any suggestion of a security role for CSCE. The four principles which NATO suggests that CSCE should work to encourage are "free and fair elections," "rule of law," "economic cooperation, based on the development of free and competitive market economies," and "cooperation on environmental protection" (London Declaration, Art. 21).

The NATO communiqué also suggests several additional improvements in CSCE that would institutionalize it and make it a more effective forum for these pursuits. Among these are regular yearly meetings and review conferences on the regularization of relations across Europe, establishment of a secretariat to serve the forum, a Center for the Prevention of Conflict, an office to monitor elections in the member nations, and a parliamentary assembly of Europe. Thus, the role that the members of NATO appear to have in mind for the CSCE is that it should become an institution where the values that make nations less of a security threat to one another might be pursued and encouraged. It is even envisioned in the communique that CSCE may have a role as discussant and perhaps referee between or among contending parties. Thus, CSCE would function as a political confidence builder, rather than having sole responsibility for security matters given to it. For the 16 members of the NATO alliance, which is half of the CSCE's membership, that function would be retained in NATO.

At the November 1990 Paris summit of the CSCE, the member nations of NATO encouraged the rest of Europe to adopt most of the goals of the NATO alliance and of the CSCE. In addition to giving the CSCE the prestige of having the CFE Treaty and the nonaggression pledge signed under its auspices, the 34 members also agreed to create a permanent secretariat to carry on the forum's affairs to be located in Prague, Czechoslovakia, and a center for conflict resolution in Vienna, Austria. Additionally, regular future meetings for foreign ministers and heads of state have been scheduled. The next summit meeting of CSCE heads of state is scheduled for Berlin, in 1992.

SECURITY IN EUROPE IN THE 1990s

The changing context in which NATO now exists, and the changing characteristics and attitudes within the alliance that are reflected in the London Declaration, will bring further change to the European security order. One possible scenario is that, despite its efforts to adjust to the new situation in Europe, NATO will follow the Warsaw Pact into irrelevance or dissolution. Central to this scenario is the reality that the Soviet threat is receding. Those who see NATO's task as having primarily, or even solely, been to defend against this threat in the past believe that its future role will be reduced as the threat is reduced. Others can envision a time in the immediate future when, because of the changes in the East, neutralism will gain ground in Germany. Consequently, it will ask the troops of its NATO partners to depart, as part of a package in which Soviet troops, by the mid-1990s, also leave their garrisons in what was East Germany. As a result, NATO, without the lion's share of its bases, and threats receding all around it, will reduce its troop strength to such minimal levels that it will recede in importance and perhaps dissolve.

Most, however, see NATO as continuing to retain a central role in Europe of the future. After all, during the key period of shifting within Europe during 1989–90, German leadership clearly chose to stay firmly anchored within the twin western organizations of NATO and the EC. The London Declaration, which the German government signed, put it this way:

> A united Germany in the Atlantic Alliance of free democracies and part of the growing political and economic integration of the European Community will be an indispensable factor of stability, which is needed in the heart of Europe. (Art. 3)

NATO is also likely to remain central in importance because the fears about the U.S.S.R., or Germany for that matter, will not recede quickly, and because NATO is appreciated for the denationalizing of defense which it has accomplished.

While continuing to play a central role, however, additional changes in the European security order may, nonetheless, occur. One possibility is that within the alliance the European members may become more independent from U.S. leadership on security matters. This would amount to the development of a "European pillar" to stand along side the American one which underpins the alliance. This tendency might be reinforced through the further development of an interest in security matters within the EC, since only Ireland among its 12 members is not also a member of NATO. The London Declaration, in fact, forthrightly recognized this possibility:

> The move within the European Community toward political union, including the development of a European identity in the domain of security, will . . . contribute to Atlantic solidarity and to the establishment of a just and lasting order of peace throughout the whole of Europe. (Art. 3)

After the Iraqi invasion of Kuwait in August 1990, the European members of NATO revitalized a little used European defense organization known as the Western European Union (WEU) and used it to coordinate their Persian Gulf military policy. Subsequently, the WEU has been suggested as a forum where Europeans might coordinate defense policy before meeting with the United States within NATO. The suggestion was made by the Italian government that the WEU should establish a formal relationship with the EC, and become, in effect, the EC's defense and security arm.

Whether the development of a European pillar within the WEU might become reality is unclear. After the outbreak of war in January 1991 in the Persian Gulf, the WEU nations ended their separate coordination and came into the war under the umbrella of American command, providing a kind of model of how a "two pillar" NATO might function. If the WEU were to become a more independent base of action for a European pillar, it would probably require a clearly defined relationship with French and British nuclear forces, and would presumably mean closer Franco-British nuclear cooperation and willingness to extend protection to the rest of European NATO. It would also probably need to be complemented by the development of an EC, rather than purely national, arms procurement policy. The implication of the evolution of a "European pillar" that would become influential within NATO would be that the United States would become less centrally involved. U.S. forces would be reduced as would the cost to the United States of

European security. NATO, however, would remain at the center of the security arrangements, despite such a potential "political" shift within it.

Whatever the internal relations of NATO, because of the decision to boost the role of the CSCE, the alliance may also begin to operate in a world in which CSCE plays an increasingly important role. Security-related matters will no doubt be discussed by CSCE, and it may well, through a center for conflict resolution, play a pivotal diplomatic role in defusing any tense situations which develop, for example, between Eastern governments over unresolved nationality claims. The NATO countries may well operate as a more or less disciplined lobby within CSCE, as all follow a line which has been preestablished, or simply influenced, by related decisions made in NATO. However, the limited effectiveness of the CSCE as a provider of security, because of its consensus decision making and lack of established military forces and command, will work to maintain a role for NATO for many years to come.

Because of these events and forces of the European security context, and the decisions incorporated into the London Declaration, the role that NATO will most likely assume for the immediate future is that of manager of change in Europe's security affairs. The alliance has taken on the role of Western clearinghouse for arms control and disarmament positions vis-à-vis the U.S.S.R. NATO has also put itself in a position of encouraging, through CSCE, the diplomatic discussion of European political and security issues and therefore will influence substantially CSCE's actions.

It is possible that the smaller CSCE members from East Europe may become members of NATO to strengthen their independence from the U.S.S.R. and to play a positive role in the security mechanism that harnesses the Germany of the future. To do so they may, to please the U.S.S.R., have to follow the East German de-militarized route. This type of security evolution might simply be a natural parallel to East Europe's closer economic association with the EC. Thus, NATO, in conjunction with the EC, might be the nucleus of a future united Europe. The Soviet Union may even find itself in the position of having to make a choice between remaining a superpower that is separate from Europe, or joining the rush to enter the

Western-originated security and economic framework as a member of Europe.

Europe's security order will no doubt change in many of the ways outlined in the London Declaration. The role and level of nuclear weapons will be reduced, as will the level of conventional forces, as continuing efforts will be made to find accommodation with the East. NATO's membership may even change, and it may be influenced by the EC, CSCE, and WEU development. But NATO, in the face of such changes, has remained a popularly supported aspect of Europe's institutional landscape. Thus, whatever else may change about European security in the next decade, it is likely that NATO will remain at the heart of those events.

BIBLIOGRAPHY

Biden, Joseph. "Helsinki II, Road Map for Revolution." *New York Times*, 28 January 1990, p. E21.

Calleo, David. *Beyond American Hegemony*. New York: Basic Books, 1987.

Davidson, Ian. "A New Alliance for a New Europe." *Financial Times* (London), 2 February 1990, p. 3.

DePorte, A. W. *Europe between the Superpowers*. (2nd ed.). New Haven: Yale University Press, 1986.

Fuerbringer, Jonathon. "Talking Deals." *New York Times*, 8 February 1990, p. D2.

Messmer, William B. "Labour's New Security Policy and Changing Europe." Unpublished research paper, 1989.

Leonard, Dick. *Pocket Guide to the European Community*. London: Economist Publications/Blackwell, 1988.

London Declaration. Final communiqué issued by NATO Heads of State Summit, London, 6 July 1990. *New York Times*, 7 July 1990, p. 7.

Norman, Peter. "UK Bids for European Development Bank HQ." *Financial Times* (London), 14 February 1990, p. 2.

Palmer, John. *Europe without America?* Oxford: Oxford University Press, 1987.

Telo, Mario. "The SPD: Between Europe and Modell Deutschland." *Telos* No. 80, Summer 1989.

Wistrich, Ernest. *After 1992, the United States of Europe*. London: Routledge, 1989, p. 105.

CHAPTER THREE

Toward a New and Invigorated United Nations

RICHARD S. RHONE

My purpose is to assess the likely role of the United Nations in the 1990s. This would be a formidable undertaking even in book length. It is all the more difficult in a brief piece such as this. In order to make the task manageable, I begin with a number of fairly basic assumptions. The United Nations, as I perceive it, is simply an elegant institutional framework within which sovereign member states go about the always difficult, often dangerous, and sometimes dirty business of international politics. It exists embedded in the larger matrix of international relations and its role cannot be understood properly in any other context. It is this larger political context which defines the actual role of the United Nations at any given moment, and the organization's role changes as the larger context changes. This being said, it remains to identify major past, present, and future trends in the larger international system and to analyze briefly their impact on an ever changing United Nations.

Below, I will outline the role of the United Nations envisaged in the charter. I will discuss briefly the impact of the Cold War and the anticolonial revolution on that role over the organization's first 40 or so years. I will assess the impact of recent revolutionary changes in the international system on the United Nations. Finally, I will attempt to anticipate the role of the organization in an increasingly complex, increasingly interdependent, and increasingly fluid international environment. I will conclude that, while the basic nature of international politics severely limited the role of the United Nations in the past, current and likely future trends in the larger international system portend an expanded, perhaps a dramatically expanded, role for the organization during the decade ahead.

Given the situation of the United Nations during much of the 1980s, this may appear to be an unreasonably optimistic conclusion. Perhaps it is. If, however, two conditions are met, an expanded U.N. role may be a distinct probability. First, the generally improving political relationships which currently characterize much of the international system must continue or, at least, must not deteriorate appreciably and irrevocably. Second, major donor states must be willing to finance the particular U.N. initiatives that they support politically. Neither is assured, but, as the organization's response to the Iraqi invasion of Kuwait seems to demonstrate, neither is out of the question.

What is assured is that there will be a substantial number of surprises, some of them unpleasant, in the years ahead and that these surprises will affect the role of the United Nations in the larger international system. The Persian Gulf war could drag on with disastrous political and economic consequences. Mikhail Gorbachev could fail and be driven from office by opponents from either his right or his left. Latent nationalistic sentiments in the Soviet Union and Eastern Europe could lead to an extremely messy period of political disintegration and realignment. The impending generation change in Chinese leadership could bring chaos. Japan and the United States could blunder into a full-fledged trade war. The ticking international debt bomb could explode. Political and budgetary pressures within the major donor states could render the United Nations financially incapable of undertaking new programs no matter how desirable they might be.

Any or all of these things, as well as a host of others, could retard substantially or even derail completely any significant expansion of the U.N.'s role. For purposes of this piece, however, I assume that such developments either will not occur or will occur in ways which do not necessarily preclude an expanded U.N. role. I assume, in other words, that the political realities of the 1990s will be difficult, but will resemble more closely the politics of the present than the politics of the past.

Richard S. Rhone

THE DISAPPOINTING PAST

The United Nations was designed primarily as a mechanism for the maintenance of international peace. This was to be achieved by means of a modified "collective security" system. In the words of Inis L. Claude, Jr., such a system involves

> the operation of a complex scheme of national commitments and international mechanisms designed to prevent or suppress aggression by any state against any other state, by presenting to potential aggressors the credible threat and to potential victims of aggression the reliable promise of effective collective measures ranging from diplomatic boycott through economic pressure to military sanctions, to enforce the peace. It was conceived as a systematic arrangement that should serve, with the highest degree of predictability that human contrivance could muster, to confront would-be aggressors, whoever they might be and wherever they might venture to strike, with an overwhelming collection of restraining power assembled by the mass of states in accordance with clear and firm obligations accepted and proclaimed in advance. (Claude, 1971, p. 247)

The provisions of the United Nations Charter relating to the maintenance of international peace and security were based upon two assumptions. First, it was assumed that the great powers (United States, Soviet Union, United Kingdom, France, China) acting in concert through the Security Council on which they hold permanent seats would be willing and able to deal with any threat to the peace. Second, it was assumed that no threat to the peace would emanate from one or more of the great powers themselves. The peace-preserving provisions of the charter, in other words, were based upon the continued unity of World War II's Big Five—what Churchill called the Grand Alliance and others have dubbed the strange alliance. The charter represented a security system to be implemented by the great powers, but not a system to be utilized against them and their individual or collective interests. Article 27, paragraph three of the charter, the Security Council's permanent-member "veto" provision, demonstrates this if proof is needed (Goodrich and Hambro, pp. 213–27).

The ink was barely dry on the charter, however, when events called into question its basic assumptions. The wartime unity of the Big Five collapsed with the onset of the Cold War. Soviet and American positions crystallized around opposing poles. The emergence of what has been termed a loose bipolar international system had a profound impact on the United Nations.

The United States came to view the United Nations as little more than a useful diplomatic tool to mobilize an anti-Soviet coalition, as it did for example during the Korean crisis of the early 1950s (see Bloomfield, pp. 41–50). The Soviets, not sitting idly by, attempted to blunt the effectiveness of U.S. efforts by means of a liberal use of their veto. Too, the Soviets attempted to use the United Nations to launch anti-Western and/or anticolonial campaigns. With some degree of success, they supported Indonesia against the Dutch, Egypt and the Sudan against the British, and Tunisia, Syria, and Lebanon against the French.

Utilizing their veto, the Soviets succeeded in bottling up Western initiatives in the Security Council. But, by means of a clever parliamentary maneuver (the "Uniting for Peace" resolution of 1950), the Western powers simply moved the Cold War struggle into the General Assembly where there was no veto and where they enjoyed an "automatic" voting majority during the early years. As Lincoln P. Bloomfield, a longtime observer of U.N. affairs, wrote,

> In the early days of the Cold War it was not uncommon for the vote in the U.N. General Assembly to be 55 to 5 on a whole range of issues. The lines were sharply drawn; the balance of power was so rigid and bipolar in structure that little flexibility for maneuver was left within the United Nations. . . . Each issue and each vote thus came to represent a separate test of free world unity. (Bloomfield, p. 8)

Richard S. Rhone

The late 1950s and early 1960s witnessed a number of important changes. Soviet hostility toward the United Nations began to soften (see Dallin, pp. 26–41). Following the 20th Party Congress which revised Stalin's "two-camp" image of the world, Moscow came to view the United Nations not just as a dangerous place where it was forced to defend itself against a permanently hostile majority, but also as a potentially fruitful arena in which to woo friends among nonaligned states in the newly recognized third camp. At the same time, U.N. membership among nonaligned states increased dramatically with the independence of an increasing number of former Western colonies. Between 1945 and 1975, the Western group of U.N. members declined from 27 percent to 18 percent of the total membership, the Latin American group declined from 41 percent to 19 percent, and the African and Asian groups increased from 20 percent to 53 percent. By 1985, the so-called Group of 77, which actually includes more than 120 developing states, represented about 75 percent of the United Nation's total membership.

These changes ushered in a transition in U.N. politics. The West's voting superiority in the General Assembly disintegrated and the United States strove mightily to reestablish it. The Soviet Union tried equally hard to establish its own stable voting majority. In short, each of the cold warriors failed and each was forced to content itself with the failure of the other. By the late 1960s to early 1970s, smaller, newer, weaker, and poorer states had become a permanent majority of U.N. members. This changed the United Nations in at least two important ways (see Claude, 1967, pp. 43–47, 62–72).

First, in matters of peace and security, the charter stressed enforcement by the great powers. The changed United Nations came to concentrate on conciliation in areas of disagreement between East and West and on peacekeeping in areas outside the immediate boundaries of the Cold War. The late United States senator, Everett Dirksen, is reputed to have had a sign on his office wall which asserted, "The oilcan is mightier than the sword!" This may not be true in all cases, but the oilcan replaced the sword as the appropriate metaphor for U.N. efforts to deal with matters affecting international peace and security. The charter's essentially coercive mechanisms of collective security were replaced almost completely in practice by the essentially persuasive methods of the third party.

The difference is critical to an understanding of the role of the United Nations in the larger international system and can be appreciated by contrasting Claude's definition of collective security quoted above with Oran R. Young's description of third-party activity as

> . . . any action taken by an actor that is not a direct party to the crisis, that is designed to reduce or remove one or more of the problems of the bargaining relationship and therefore to facilitate the termination of the crisis itself . . . The role is basically persuasive rather than coercive in the sense that it does not involve the direct use of military force. . . . The role is ultimately directed toward aiding the parties to a crisis to realize their own common or overlapping interests when various problems threaten to disrupt or severely downgrade their bargaining relationship. In this sense the third party attempts to help both sides rather than to tip the balance toward one or the other. (Young, pp. 34–35)

Second, the U.N. Charter embodied the traditional view that matters of "high politics" deserved first place on the international agenda. It was assumed that peace and security issues, especially those of particular interest to the major powers, would command a majority of the time and resources of an organization like the United Nations. The new majority of U.N. members which emerged in the 1960s didn't see it that way. Once in control of the U.N.'s agenda, if not most of its resources, the newer members were for the most part content to leave the details of the Cold War to the cold warriors and pushed the United Nations in the direction of those issues which affected *them* most directly. Increasingly, North-South issues like anticolonialism, self-determination, economic development and the establishment of a "new international economic order" moved to center stage in the General Assembly and, in some cases, in the Security Council as well. These kinds of issues remain center stage today.

All of this demonstrates that the United Nations does not exist in a political vacuum. Its role is shaped and reshaped, often profoundly, by major political forces in the larger international system. This is not about to change, and in that sense the organization is no different today than it was at its inception. In the same sense, it is no different today than it will be during the rest of the 1990s. It will continue to change as international politics changes. Therefore, it remains to identify major shifts currently influencing the shape and direction of global politics and to assess briefly their impact on the United Nations.

THE CHANGED AND CHANGING PRESENT

To be sure, politics along both the East-West and North-South axes continues to define much of the U.N.'s role in the global system. But two recent changes in intra-axis dynamics, one obvious and dramatic and the other not so obvious but equally dramatic, have altered and probably enhanced that role substantially. I refer to the loudly proclaimed, and perhaps now actual, demise of the Cold War on the one hand and the more gradual and less visible global triumph of market over centrally planned economies on the other. Both have influenced the United Nations and, barring a complete reversal of current trends in international politics and political economy, that influence is likely to continue and increase.

There is currently greater active cooperation between the United States and the Soviet Union than at any time in the checkered history of superpower relations within (and without) the United Nations. This increased cooperation extends as well to the other three permanent members of the Security Council on a whole range of issues and has led to a substantial number of recent "successes" and a Nobel Peace Prize for the U.N. Superpower cooperation in the United Nations has been rare but it is not without precedent. Soviet-American consultations both inside and outside the United Nations, for instance, made possible the organization's role in helping to terminate and maintain a cessation of hostilities in the 1973 Middle Eastern war. What is unprecedented is the sheer number of recent cases in which superpower cooperation has made possible an enhanced U.N. role in the amelioration of some of the world's seemingly most intractable conflicts.

The list is impressive. The situation in Western Sahara seems to be on its way to a solution with the help of the secretary-general. United Nations personnel helped to negotiate, and subsequently observed, the Soviet withdrawal from Afghanistan, and a good-offices mission remains to iron out lingering difficulties between Afghanistan and Pakistan. A cease-fire was arranged in the Iran-Iraq war under the good offices of the secretary-general, and a peacekeeping mission is on site to supervise and maintain it. A group of U.N. observers in Nicaragua aided in assuring a free and fair election. A United Nations transition-assistance group helped to conduct the recent elections in Namibia and remained to smooth the way to independence while a verification mission was in Angola to monitor the withdrawal of Cuban troops. None of this could have happened without the cooperation of the superpowers and the approval of the Security Council's other three permanent members.

It is significant that the initiatives noted above were begun before the most recent dramatic changes involving Eastern Europe and the Soviet Union's various republics. If such things were possible in the context of a mere thaw in superpower relations, the apparently imminent meltdown of the Cold War raises some extremely interesting possibilities for an increased U.N. role in the short-to-medium-term settlement of a number of other seemingly intractable problems as well. Cambodia is a case in point.

The 20-year-old Cambodia conflict is notable for a number of reasons. It has become a perennial item on the U.N.'s agenda. So far, it has defied solution—indeed it has often seemed to defy rational analysis. All of the Security Council's permanent members have had conflicting and apparently shifting interests in the outcome. In short, Cambodia will be an extremely tough nut to crack. Yet it appears that the conflict may be progressing by fits and starts toward a solution and that the United Nations will play a major role in that solution on the recommendation of all five permanent members. They have agreed that "an effective U.N. presence will be required" to verify the withdrawal of foreign forces, supervise elections, and otherwise ease the transition to a democratically elected government (*New York Times*, 17 January 1990, pp. A1, A6) and have authored a comprehensive settlement plan which would involve "transferring temporary control of the country to the United Nations" (*New York*

Times, 29 August 1990, p. A1). Difficulties remain, but it is significant that they arise in no small part from differences over the precise size and shape of U.N. involvement in what many now seem to assume will be an eventual solution to the conflict.

More significant than the longer-term possibilities of the Cambodia case, however, are the immediate realities of the U.N. response to Iraq's invasion of Kuwait—a response potentially as important for the future of the organization as the lack of substantial response to the Japanese invasion of Manchuria and the Italian invasion of Ethiopia were for the League of Nations. The importance of Security Council Resolution 661 and 678 (see Appendix) which imposed comprehensive economic sanctions on and authorized military action against Iraq cannot be overestimated.

These actions are enforcement measures under Chapter VII of the charter and are, in theory at least, mandatory for all U.N. members. Chapter VII initiatives, the most vigorous type of action possible under the charter, have been extremely rare and of questionable effectiveness as a result of basic political cleavages in the larger international system. In this case, however, sanctions were adopted with the concurrence of all of the Security Council's permanent members (China abstained on Resolution 678) and a substantial majority of the remaining ten nonpermanent members. The speed and vigor of the U.N. response to this crisis along with the initial level of international support for that response are unprecedented and serve to demonstrate that the organization might indeed approximate rather closely the role envisaged in the charter if global conditions are right.

The sanctions, however, are a double-edged sword. If they result in a reasonably rapid withdrawal of Iraq from Kuwait and peace in Persian Gulf region, it will constitute the most significant of the U.N.'s recent successes. That would bode well for the future of the organization. If, on the other hand, the crisis drags on inclusively, if support for the sanctions weakens, if the operation loses its international character, or if the effort to dislodge Iraq from Kuwait fails entirely, Resolutions 661 and 678 could become the latest additions to an unfortunately substantial list of ambitious but largely unfulfilled United Nations resolutions. That, of course, would bode ill for the future of the organization.

It is not at all certain at this writing if or how the situation in the Persian Gulf will be resolved. Whatever the outcome, however, it is certain that the United Nations will be a different place, for good or ill, as a result.

Nevertheless, it appears that the permanent members are developing the habit of meeting both inside and outside the U.N. on an increasingly regular basis for the purpose of forging solutions to a whole range of contentious issues. In New York, they have institutionalized the process and it appears that the United Nations figures in an increasingly prominent way in the implementation of those solutions. Given the state of permanent-member relations and their tendency to avoid the United Nations whenever possible over the last four and one-half decades, this is nothing short of astounding. Just a few short years ago, for instance, the recent U.S. call for an expanded U.N. peacekeeping role in Nicaragua (*New York Times*, 10 March 1990, p. 5), as well as the sanctions imposed by the Security Council on Iraq would have been absolutely unthinkable.

In the words of Secretary-General Javier Pérez de Cuéllar, "The benevolence of the political climate and the general will to pragmatic action have never been so evident" (*U.N. Chronicle*, p. 38). Barring a reversal of current trends in the larger international system, increased reliance on U.N. machinery is likely to continue as long as international problems and the will to solve them remain. There is simply no other international instrument as well-equipped as the United Nations to do much of what the major powers apparently want done but can't, for a variety of reasons, do by themselves at this point in time.

Strange as it may seem, these developments may not be an entirely unmixed blessing (*New York Times*, 5 August 1990, p. E3). Closer cooperation among the Security Council's permanent members has upset the rather elaborate behind-the-scenes consultation procedures which have evolved over the past three decades and have allowed the council to function as well as it has (see Chai). Nonaligned members of the council have begun to hold meetings of their own in order to outline common positions to counter what some regard as the permanent members' excessive assertiveness. It is not certain where all of this will lead, but it appears that some adjustments in the council's procedures will be necessary to accommodate the changing patterns of permanent and nonpermanent member interaction. Juergen Dedring, a member of the secretary-general's recently created Office of Research and the Collection of Information (ORCI), summarizes the situation:

> While this new phenomenon does indeed recall the original special responsibility of the permanent members, there is little doubt that the evolution of the international system in more than 40 years of United Nations history has opened a huge gap between the theory of the Charter and the current practice. The jury is still out on the question whether the exclusive and privileged role of the five veto powers is an anachronism or the wave of the future in the emerging global order. (Dedring, p. 11)

Changes on the economic front have not been so apparent, but they have been taking place, their direction has become clear, and their influence has been felt in the United Nations. The virtual collapse of the economies of Eastern Europe and the collapsing economy of the Soviet Union only serve to accelerate existing trends. In spite of the apparent reluctance of some to acknowledge publicly what has now become obvious, market economies have not only been winning the battle with their centrally planned counterparts in the global marketplace. They have also been winning the battle in the United Nations for the minds and now perhaps even the hearts of increasing numbers of previously unconvinced members. In the words of Felix Rohatyn,

> The ideological walls are crumbling all over the world. The basic national objectives in both the communist and the free worlds consist of sustained economic growth, greater competitiveness, and higher standards of living. The global divisions that continue to exist, and that will become more and more serious, will be between haves and have nots, rich and poor, competitive and inadequate. Such distinctions, however, will no longer be primarily ideological in source. (Rohatyn, p. 54)

The bulk of the membership of the Group of 77 has not really objected to quiet shifts in the approach of U.N. agencies to accommodate this new economic situation. Two examples illustrate the point. First, the U.N.'s Centre on Transnational Corporations began with the primary purpose of helping developing host countries protect themselves from what were widely perceived to be the less than desirable effects of transnationals. This function remains, but the emphasis has changed. Today, the Centre spends much of its time and most of its resources helping to forge mutually beneficial relationships between transnational corporations and potential host countries in the developing world. The generally positive experience of the newly industrializing countries (NICs) of the Pacific Basin, it seems, has not gone unnoticed.

> What . . . has changed over the years is the international climate, and that cannot but affect the work of the Centre. During the 1970s, developing countries . . . were denouncing the "imperialist exploitation" of multinational corporations and pressing hard for the establishment of a new, more equitable, global economic order. Now these same countries, crippled by debt and disillusioned by the failure of some of their experiments in alternative development, are courting the multinationals. (Caplan, p. 14)

Second, there has been a similar but less pronounced shift in the approach of the United Nations Development Programme (UNDP), the organization's principal provider of technical assistance to developing countries. While UNDP must respond to the actual requests of recipient states and cannot dictate policy to them, it can influence subtly the kinds of projects for which potential recipients are likely to request funding. Simply put, UNDP has been reducing progressively the emphasis on larger public-sector projects and increasing the emphasis on more "people-oriented" or private-sector projects. It has come to view the latter as more likely contributors to sustainable long-term development. Significantly, this has caused very few problems. A majority of recipients, it appears, are now thinking, if not always speaking publicly, along the same lines.

While the effects of these and other similar changes on the role of the United Nations are neither as obvious as those occasioned by the political changes noted above nor as likely to produce immediate and tangible results, they are certainly not insignificant. The near-term result is likely to be a continued lowering of voices as the General Assembly debates the many questions of global economics and economic development which appear yearly on its agenda. The angry rhetoric which characterized much of the debate surrounding the issue of the establishment of a New International Economic Order (NIEO) from the mid-1970s to the mid-1980s has abated considerably. "The more cooperative atmosphere within the Security Council is rubbing off on the General Assembly" (*New York Times*, 5 August 1990, p. E3). Recent events in the larger international political economy have served to clear away much of the rhetorical and ideological underbrush which has retarded the potential role of the United Nations in the solution of any number of the world's pressing economic and social problems. "Three years ago," says the secretary-general, "this would have seemed to many to be an idle dream" (*UN Chronicle*, p. 39).

It is not certain that the U.N.'s potential in any or all of these areas will be realized fully, especially in the short run. However, some realization of that potential is no longer unthinkable. Indeed, it is probably inevitable over the longer haul given the changing nature of the political map.

THE CAUTIOUSLY OPTIMISTIC FUTURE

There are other more fundamental forces at work which portend not only profound long-run changes in the very nature of the international system but also significant changes for the role of the United Nations in that system. Several familiar examples illustrate the more general point. Decisions made in Tokyo's boardrooms affect directly the job security of large numbers of American workers. Decisions made by Peruvian farmers to grow coca leaves rather than corn have a direct impact on the murder rate in Washington, D.C. Patterns of electric power consumption in the upper Midwest affect Canadian-American relations much as poverty south of the Rio

Grande affects Mexican-American relations. Decisions in Argentina, Mexico, and Brazil to repay or to default on loans have a direct impact on the stability of the American banking system. The list could go on and on.

Each of these examples represents a basic political problem that could easily affect the long-term security interests of the United States. As such, each represents a problem that demands a solution. To be sure, they are not the kinds of "security" problems which the United States has come to know and love, but security problems they remain. The threats come from unaccustomed sources and arise out of issues not previously considered threatening. What is more, the fact that the United States has a vast nuclear arsenal is absolutely irrelevant to the solution of these and a host of other similar problems. They will have to be solved by means of negotiated agreements, not by traditional methods of power politics, and actors not previously considered "powerful" will be increasingly influential parties to the negotiations. The United States is, of course, not alone in this. All states confront the same kind of unfamiliar political landscape.

Robert O. Keohane and Joseph S. Nye describe the basic outlines of this kind of changed and changing international system in which traditional power politics is progressively replaced by a politics of "complex interdependence" (see Keohane and Nye, pp. 3–60). A detailed discussion of their excellent work is clearly beyond the scope of this analysis. Suffice to say, they describe a system in which "international regimes" play an increasingly vital role and in which international organizations play an expanded role in the maintenance, alteration, and/or creation of such regimes.

International regimes are "sets of implicit or explicit principles, norms, rules and decision-making procedures around which actors' expectations converge in a given area of international relations" (Krasner, p. 186). They are the implicitly or explicitly accepted "rules of the game" without which much of international life could easily degenerate into an unmitigated Hobbesian brawl. Keohane clarifies the concept of regimes:

> Principles, norms, rules, and procedures all contain injunctions about behavior; they prescribe certain actions

and proscribe others. They imply obligations, even though these obligations are not enforceable through a hierarchical legal system. It clarifies the definition of regime, therefore, to think of it in terms of injunctions of greater or lesser specificity. Some are far-reaching and extremely important. They may change only rarely. At the other extreme, injunctions may be merely technical, matters of convenience that can be altered without great political or economic impact. In-between are injunctions that are both specific enough that violations of them are in principle identifiable and that changes in them can be observed, and sufficiently significant that changes in them make a difference for the behavior of actors. . . . It is these intermediate injunctions—politically consequential but specific enough that violations and changes can be identified—that I take as the essence of international regimes. (Keohane, p. 59)

The international system has always had regimes, often imposed by hegemonic powers, and they are still vital, but that may be the only thing about them that hasn't changed and isn't changing. The "important" issue areas of international relations, those areas which are widely perceived to affect directly the basic, long-term security interests of states, have increased dramatically in number and scope. The ranks of hegemons capable of imposing their individual will in given issue areas is thinning rapidly. Traditional hegemons are increasingly forced to negotiate with newly "powerful" actors in a host of newly urgent issue areas. One only need consider the roles of Saudi Arabia in relation to international energy questions, Japan in relation to international trade questions, and Colombia, Bolivia, and Peru in relation to the emerging narcotic drug regime to illustrate this.

What does all of this portend for the United Nations? If Keohane and Nye are correct in postulating an increasing importance for international regimes and an expanding role for organizations in the management of those regimes—and there is mounting evidence they are correct on both counts—we might expect to see a growing role for the United Nations in the years ahead. It is important to note that this role, while expanded, will not be an entirely unfamiliar one. It is precisely the kind of role that the United Nations has been playing, albeit quietly, for quite some time. The organization's pioneering work in relation to the existing human rights, oceans, and outer space regimes, for example, attests to this.

There are any number of areas in which existing regimes appear to be ripe for alteration or strengthening. In many of these areas, United Nations machinery or U.N. related specialized agencies are already in place, and there is no reason to believe that states will choose to "re-invent the wheel" as they are increasingly forced to find appropriate fora in which to negotiate collective solutions to their common problems. For instance, I think we might expect to see expanded roles for the Disarmament Commission, the International Atomic Energy Agency, the World Health Organization, the World Bank, and the International Monetary Fund in relation to those regimes falling within their respective areas of competence. Indeed, the roles of the latter two institutions have expanded already in relation to the international debt crisis.

Beyond this, there are an increasing number of problem areas which seem to demand the creation of international regimes—problem areas which have begun to impact the more broadly defined security interests of increasing numbers of states. Who would argue, for instance, that the problems of narcotic drug trafficking, the environment, or refugees have not become so serious as to affect the security interests of increasing numbers of states, large and small? Who would argue today that unilateral or bilateral action will be adequate to solve them? The United Nations has been dealing with these issues too, but comprehensive and detailed international rules of the game have yet to be negotiated. There is little doubt that such agreed rules will eventually emerge. The national interest of states increasingly demands it. Too, it is increasingly probable that existing U.N. machinery—the Commission on Narcotic Drugs, the United Nations Environment Programme, the Office of the United Nations High Commissioner for Refugees, the General Assembly, and perhaps even the Security Council—or agencies yet to be created will play an expanded role not only in the negotiation process but also in the management of the resulting regimes.

I do not wish to convey the impression that the process of regime creation, modification, and maintenance either inside or outside the United Nations will necessarily bring quick or easy results. To be sure, it will not. There is a great deal of extremely hard bargaining ahead, and near-to-medium-term successes are by no means assured. One need only look to the recently concluded 17th special session of the General Assembly called to address the issue of illicit narcotic drugs in order to illustrate the problems as well as the prospects.

The narcotic drug problem has clearly become an issue which affects not only the internal security of growing numbers of individual states but also relations between states. Before the problem can be solved, it must be defined. Is it a problem of demand or is it a problem of supply? Do producer nations or consumer nations bear the primary responsibility for the problem and its solution? Who should foot the huge bill for an ultimate solution? The Colombian representative at the 17th special session put it succinctly:

> The 1980s were marked by a lack of leadership in dealing with this extremely delicate matter and by a failure to face up to the responsibility incumbent upon each State in the fight against this scourge. Instead, there was a widespread and simplistic notion that the countries producing and processing the coca plant were the ones that should be seeking, alone and at all costs, a solution to the problem. . . . Similarly, the determined and even heroic struggle of some countries to eliminate the trafficking and processing of narcotic drugs will serve no purpose if at the same time no action is taken against the export of precursor chemicals; if no action is taken to discourage consumption; if there is no control over the transport of the additives and base products needed to manufacture drugs; if there is no proper control of the production of raw materials; if no effective action is taken against corrupt officials and civilian, military and police authorities in certain countries who, through their action or inaction, promote trafficking in narcotic and precursor substances; if no legal action is

taken against property and nothing is done to prevent the laundering of monies derived from those activities; if there is no close cooperation with States that have taken up the struggle and if there is no just and equitable assistance of the economies of the developing countries most affected by drug production and processing. (GAOR, A/S-17/PV.1. pp. 26–27)

These issues and a host of others must be addressed before there can be any hope of a solution to the larger problem. They are intensely political issues which require negotiated solutions. Victory in the "war" on drugs, in short, will require an international narcotic drug regime which clearly prescribes and proscribes certain kinds of state behavior. Too, it will require some kind of international machinery to monitor the performance of states.

Recent events which culminated in the 17th special session of the General Assembly indicate that the broad outlines of a narcotic drug regime are emerging and that the United Nations, in addition to providing a principal international forum for the negotiation of drug issues, will play a major role in the management of that regime. Building on the December 1988 United Nations Convention Against Illicit Traffic in Narcotic Drugs and Psychotropic Substances (ECOSOCOR, E/CONF. 82/15) and the February 1990 Cartagena Declaration by the Presidents of Bolivia, Colombia, Peru, and the United States (GAOR, A/S-17/8), the 17th special session adopted unanimously a comprehensive and reasonably detailed Global Programme of Action to deal with narcotic drugs (GAOR, A/RES/S-17/2).

Significantly, the Programme of Action was accompanied by a political declaration which indicates basic agreement that

the fight against illicit trafficking in narcotic drugs and psychotropic substances has to comprise effective measures aimed ... at eliminating illicit consumption, cultivation, and production of narcotic drugs and psychotropic substances; preventing the diversion from legitimate uses of precursor chemicals, specific substances, materials and equipment frequently used in the illicit manufacture of narcotic drugs and psychotropic substances; and preventing the use of the banking system and other financial institutions for the laundering of proceeds derived from illicit drug trafficking by making such activities criminal offenses. (GAOR, A/RES/S-17/2, p. 3)

The agreements reached at the 17th special session touch all of the relative bases and were achieved only after much difficult negotiation and many compromises. Indeed, the choice of the General Assembly as the forum to deal with the issue was itself the product of some hard bargaining. The United States and Britain would have preferred to address the narrower questions of interdiction and eradication in the more intimate and manageable Security Council (*New York Times*, 21 February 1990, p. A3). But the issue was bargained into the larger General Assembly and, as a result, all parties now have a reasonably clear indication of their own obligations as well as the obligations of others. All have given something in order to get something of value and it will be extremely difficult for any state to reap the benefits of the agreements without shouldering its fair share of the burden of implementing them.

To be sure, the final chapters of the international community's struggle against narcotic drugs remain to be written. Many details must still be worked out and much additional hard bargaining looms. Problems along the border between the United States and Mexico illustrate the kinds of difficulties which will have to be dealt with on a global scale. Responding to what it perceives to be Mexico's unwillingness to coordinate antidrug efforts along the border, the United States has established a drug task force under the command of the U.S. Army. Mexico "has expressed alarm to Washington at what it sees as growing militarization of the border" and a potential threat to its sovereignty (*New York Times*, 25 February 1990, p. 18). The depth of Mexican concern is evident in the words of its representative at the 17th special session:

We repeat that the fight against drug trafficking must be carried out with scrupulous respect for each country's national sovereignty. . . . We insist on . . . a comprehensive, balanced approach to the fight against drug production, abuse and trafficking. . . . Unilateral measures, arbitrary positions that slander and intimidate, threats that offend the sovereignty of peoples and the dignity of individuals, cannot be tolerated. (GAOR, A/S-17/PV.1, p. 51)

In spite of the fact that the rights and obligations of both the United States and Mexico were clarified at the 17th special session, it remains to define the precise kinds of actions which constitute legitimate protection of those rights and good faith efforts to fulfill those obligations. It will not be easy.

Nevertheless, the same kinds of forces in the larger international system which made possible the current expanded role of the United Nations in the peace and security field have opened the possibilities for an increased role for the United Nations in a host of other areas like narcotic drugs. The emerging political imperatives of complex interdependence seem to portend such an expanded role—not because states see the United Nations as an alternative to their national interests but precisely because they see the United Nations as an increasingly useful and even necessary mechanism for the protection of these now more broadly defined interests.

CONCLUSION

In one sense, we end where we began. Politics in the larger international system defined the role of the United Nations in the late 1940s and continued to define that role through the late 1980s. In will continue to define the organization's role well into the 21st century. In a more important sense, however, we end in a vastly different place. While the process by which the international system defines the role of the United Nations persists, the end product of that process is dramatically different today as a result of fundamental changes in the dynamics of the larger international system and promises to be even more so in the years ahead if present trends are not reversed.

In the past, a combination of forces produced an essentially hostile international environment in which the role of the United

Nations was marginal at best and irrelevant at worst. Frankly, there was very little incentive in such an environment for states to resort to the United Nations if they could not utilize its machinery against their opponents or to further their own narrowly construed national interests and, since roughly the mid-1960s, it has not been possible for any state or group of states to do so consistently and effectively. Therefore, it is no wonder that the United Nations often found itself condemned to the periphery of international politics and teetering on the brink of bankruptcy.

The situation has changed substantially in recent years and appears to be changing more rapidly with each passing day. Major impediments to international cooperation on both the East-West and North-South axes have dissolved or seem to be dissolving. Indeed, the boundaries of the axes themselves are becoming increasingly blurred. At the same time, increasingly urgent international problems which national leaders themselves now believe require multilaterally negotiated solutions abound. In short, the price to be paid by states for a lack of international cooperation has become increasingly unacceptable while the benefits to be derived from such cooperation are becoming increasingly obvious. The role of the United Nations can do nothing except expand in scope and significance in such an international climate—but many funny and not so funny things can still happen on the way to this particular forum.

BIBLIOGRAPHY

Bloomfield, Lincoln P. *The United Nations and U.S. Foreign Policy.* Boston: Little, Brown and Company, 1960.

Caplan, Richard. "Tracking Transnationals: United Nations Centre on Transnational Corporations." *Multinational Monitor*, July/August, 1989.

Chai, F.Y. *Consultation and Consensus in the Security Council.* New York: United Nations Institute for Training and Research, 1971.

Claude, Inis L., Jr. *The Changing United Nations.* New York: Random House, 1967..

Claude, Inis L., Jr. *Swords into Plowshares: The Problems and Progress of International Organization.* 4th ed. New York: Random House, 1971.

Dallin, Alexander. *The Soviet Union at the United Nations.* New York: Frederick A. Praeger, 1962.

Dedring, Juergen. "Towards Greater Effectiveness of the Security Council." *United Nations Institute for Training and Research (UNITAR) Newsletter* (November/December, 1989).

Goodrich, Leland M. and Hambro, Edvard. *Charter of the United Nations: Commentary and Documents.* Revised ed. Boston: World Peace Foundation, 1949.

Keohane, Robert O. *After Hegemony: Cooperation and Discord in the World Political Economy.* Princeton: Princeton University Press, 1984.

Keohane, Robert O. and Nye, Joseph S. *Power and Interdependence.* second ed. Boston: Scott, Foresman and Company, 1989.

Krasner, Stephen D. "Structural Causes and Regime Consequences: Regimes as Intervening Variables," *International Organization* 36 (Spring 1982).

Rohatyn, Felix. "America's Economic Dependence." *Foreign Affairs* (1989), no. 1.

The New York Times. 17 January 1990; 21 February 1990; 25 February 1990; 10 March 1990; 10 March 1990; 5 August 1990; 29 August 1990.

U.N. Chronicle. 26 (December 1989).

United Nations Economic and Social Council Official Records (cited ECOSOCOR). E/CONF.82/15, 19 December 1988.

United Nations General Assembly Official Records (cited GAOR). A/S-17/8, 21 February 1990; A/RES/S-17/2, 15 March 1990; A/S-17/PV.1, 23 February 1990.

Young, Oran R. *The Intermediaries: Third Parties in International Crises.* Princeton: Princeton University Press, 1967.

CHAPTER FOUR

Violent Conflict in the International System of the 1990s

DOUGLAS W. SIMON

INTRODUCTION

On 2 August 1990, the military forces of Iraq brutally invaded the tiny country of Kuwait. Five months later, a coalition of 25 countries led by the United States began military operations to expel Saddam Hussein's occupying forces from the tiny oil sheikdom. The coalition's initial blow against Iraq was the largest aerial bombing campaign in history.

It was as if these grim events jarred our sense of reality. Political developments in the latter half of the 1980s led us to believe that we might experience a significant reduction in the number and intensity of violent international conflicts. Tensions between the United States and the Soviet Union had lessened considerably. The Intermediate Nuclear Force Treaty (INF) of 1988 eliminated an entire class of nuclear weapons. The superpowers agreed in principle to a drastic reduction of strategic nuclear weapons and both announced conventional force reductions in Europe and appeared intent on continuing that process through negotiation. Smarting from the Vietnam and Afghanistan experiences, American and Soviet decisionmakers seemed intent on reducing their direct and prolonged interventions into Third World conflicts. The Eastern bloc crumbled before the world's eyes as Communist party after Communist party in Eastern Europe relinquished power. Western Europe was embarked on a far-reaching plan for economic integration sometime in the early 1990s. Finally, through a combination of big power politics and the efforts of a rejuvenated United Nations, several international conflicts ended or were near conclusion—Namibia, the Spanish Sahara, and the Iran-Iraq war.

As encouraging as these developments are and as the Persian Gulf war illustrates, it would be naive to believe that they somehow signal a drastic reduction in violent international conflict. While the superpowers appear to have grown weary of fighting and/or heavily funding guerrilla wars, and ideology no longer provides a primary motivating force for a great deal of international tension, a close look at the international system reveals that violence within and between states is as prevalent as ever and will continue into the foreseeable future. The demise of communism and the spread of democratic systems does not mean that nation-states will somehow stop seeking to insure their self-interests and if necessary to defend those interests by violent means. Many of today's conflicts find, and will continue to find, their origins in strong and long-standing nationalistic and ethnic tensions. One of the primary contentions of this paper is that over the next decade we are likely to see an increase in the propensity of culturally-based minority groups within nation-states to seek violently to fulfill their aspirations for self-rule. It is important to note that these ethnically based conflicts will not be confined to the Third World. The spread of pluralism in Eastern Europe and the Soviet Union has already facilitated considerable ethnic conflict.

A second type of violent conflict that we are likely to experience with greater frequency is the antidrug war, fought within and between states.

Moreover, the 1990 Iraqi invasion of Kuwait clearly demonstrates that the decade will probably see its share of classic aggression for the simple purpose of enhancing state power.

The future of religious wars, or the jihad, is a bit more in doubt. It is very popular to assert that since the Iranian revolution and the rise of the Ayatollah Khomeini, militant Islam has been on the march. This paper will argue that while Islamic fundamentalism is a legitimate concern, there are serious doubts about predictions of holy wars emanating out of the Middle East.

Feeding the areas of violent conflict are a growing number of developing nations entering the arms business, not only sales, but production. The increasing use of chemical weapons as well as the race for ballistic missiles by Third World nations are ominous developments. Finally, we can expect terrorism most certainly to be part of the international political landscape of the 1990s.

THE FREQUENCY OF VIOLENT CONFLICT

Data gathered by Singer and Small certainly does not support the notion that the frequency of collective international violence has been declining in recent decades. To the contrary, while their long-term studies dating from 1815 do not reveal any discernible pattern of either greater or lesser number of conflicts, data for the three-decade period of 1950 to 1980 does reveal an increase in the frequency of violent conflict (see Table I). This is particularly true if one includes both interstate and civil wars with battle deaths in excess of 1,000 (Small and Singer, 1982, pp. 203–204; Small and Singer, 1984, pp. 26–37).

Using Singer and Small's criteria, a quick perusal of the news of the 1980s reveals that no less than 22 violent civil wars of varying intensity raged on and off throughout the decade—Burma, East Timor, Chad, Kampuchea, Uganda, Mozambique, Colombia, Northern Ireland, and Peru, as well as the carry-over conflicts from the 1970s, including Afghanistan, Angola, El Salvador, Ethiopia, Guatemala, India (Sikh), Lebanon, Nicaragua, the Philippines, Somalia, Sudan, Sri Lanka, and the Western Sahara. Interstate conflicts either broke out or continued between Iran and Iraq, Argentina and the United Kingdom, Syria and Lebanon for a total of 25, near the figure for the 1970s and higher than the decades of the 1950s and 1960s. Many of these conflicts remain unresolved and will no doubt carry into the 1990s and beyond. If one uses less restrictive criteria for defining interstate and civil war, 71 states faced some sort of insurgency between 1980 and 1988 (Boswell, p. 1). New conflicts will no doubt emerge during the decade of the 1990s. In

TABLE I

INTERNATIONAL AND CIVIL WARS 1950-1980

1950-1959	1960-1969	1970-1979
Korean (I)	Sino-India (I)	Bangladesh (I)
Algerian (C)	Vietnamese (I)	Philippine (C)
Russo-Hungarian (I)	Second Kashmir (I)	Yom Kippur (I)
Sinai (I)	Six Day War (I)	Turko-Cypr. (I)
Tibetan (C)	Israeli-Egyptian (I)	Viet-Cambod. (I)
Algeria (Ci)	Honduras-El Salv. (I)	Saharan (I)
Argentina (Ci)	Algeria (Ci)	Afghanistan (Ci)
Bolivia (Ci)	China (Ci)	Angola (Ci)
Burma (Ci)	Colombia (Ci)	Cambodia (Ci)
China (Ci)	Dom. Republic (Ci)	El Salvador (Ci)
Colombia (Ci)	India (Ci)	Ethiopia (Ci)
Cuba (Ci)	Laos (Ci)	Guatemala (Ci)
Indonesia (Ci)	Nigeria (Ci)	Indonesia (Ci)
Iraq (Ci)	Rwanda (Ci)	Iran (Ci)
Laos (Ci)	Sudan (Ci)	Jordan (Ci)
Lebanon (Ci)	Uganda (Ci)	Laos (Ci)
Philippines (Ci)	Vietnam (Ci)	Lebanon (Ci)
Vietnam (Ci)	Yemen (Ci)	Nicaragua (Ci)
Guatemala (Ci)	Zaire (Ci)	Nigeria (Ci)
		Pakistan (Ci)
		Philippines (Ci)
		Somalia (Ci)
		Sudan (Ci)
		Sri Lanka (Ci)
		Vietnam (Ci)
		West Sahara (Ci)
		Zimbabwe (Ci)

I = Interstate War
C = Colonial War
Ci = Civil War

Source: Melvin Small and J. David Singer, *Resort to Arms: International Civil Wars 1816-1980*, Beverly Hills, CA: Sage Publications, 1982; and Melvin Small and J. David Singer, "Patterns in International Warfare, 1816-1980," in Small and Singer, *International War: An Anthology*, second edition, Chicago: The Dorsey Press, 1984, pp. 26-37.

1990, a vicious civil war broke out in Liberia, and in the Middle East the military forces of Iraq's Saddam Hussein invaded the tiny oil-rich country of Kuwait.

VIOLENT CONFLICTS OF THE 1990s

The advent of the 1990s signals the end of two dominant forms of conflict—ideological and anticolonial. As Evan Luard points out, the great "Wars of Ideology" date from 1917. From the end of World War I to the present we have seen the totalitarian creeds of Germany, Italy, and Japan rise and fall, followed by the intense conflict between the democratic capitalist Western powers and the Marxist-Leninist ideas of the Soviet bloc during the Cold War. Parallel and sometimes intertwined with the titanic East-West ideological battle were the anticolonial wars of the 1950s and 1960s.

The advent of the 1990s signals the end of these two dominant forms of conflict—ideological and anticolonial. In addition to the potential for recurrent violence in traditional conflict areas such as the Middle East, the decade will witness a surge in ethnic violence and an increase in drug wars as governments attempt to stem the production and flow of illegal narcotics.

Ethnic Wars

An ethnic minority is defined as a group of people who differ from a dominant group by virtue of language, race, color, national, religious, or cultural origins. The group may or may not suffer from persecution and/or discrimination.* The struggle of ethnic minorities to fulfill their expectations for autonomy or independence will intensify in the next decade.

---

*There is considerable agreement as to what constitutes an ethnic group as well as an ethnic minority. Any number of standard reference works list a surprisingly large number of factors that can define what is ethnic. See: *Webster's Ninth New Collegiate Dictionary, The World Book Encyclopedia, The World Encyclopedia of Peace.*

Of course, ethnic rebellions and liberation movements have existed for centuries. For the past few decades these conflicts have often been caused by the arbitrary state lines formed by the colonial powers which either divided national communities or isolated them as persecuted minorities, a particularly acute problem in Africa. Some of these conflicts have been especially brutal. In East Timor in the Indonesian archipelago, over 90,000 civilians have been massacred or died of war-related famine since 1975 (Merida, pp. 3M–4M). In Uganda, ethnic and tribal violence has resulted in the deaths of over 100,000 since the fall of Idi Amin in the 1970s. In Mozambique, 100,000 died in 1987–88 alone during what has been a 14-year war between the central government and the rebel forces of RENAMO (Mozambique National Resistance). Sri Lanka seems caught up in a terrible cycle of ethnic violence between the Tamil and Sinhalese communities, as does India with its Hindu-Sikh war in the Punjab (Merida, pp. 3M–4M). What is alarming is that the potential for this type of conflict expanding seems almost limitless. In the Appendix of this chapter is a list of major ethnic groups around the world that have in recent years taken some political action to assert national identity, ethnic sovereignty, territorial claims, and/or to insure their very survival as a distinct culture. Many of the acts have been non-violent and within the law. Nevertheless, given the current political climate, each region in which these groups exists is a danger spot for real and potential violence.

There are few regions of the world free from this renewed ethnic consciousness. Until recently, most of the post–World War II conflicts were fought in the Third World. Yet in Europe, most notably in multicultural societies such as Yugoslavia and the Soviet Union, the potential for widespread violence is ever present. In fact, the Soviet Union in recent years has been racked by ethnically based protests and violent conflict, most notably in the Baltic republics of Lithuania, Estonia, and Latvia, and in the province of Nagorno-Karabakh between Christian Armenians and Muslim Azerbaijanis. The "nationalities problem" as it is called in the U.S.S.R. is particularly hazardous for Mikhail Gorbachev and the current Kremlin leadership. As the Appendix of this chapter indicates, at least 15 ethnic trouble spots are readily identifiable within the Soviet Union.

Douglas W. Simon

What forces are at work that threaten to distinguish the 1990s as the decade of global ethnic violence? In most cases the ethnic tensions are decades, and in some cases, centuries old. The question is, why now should they emerge with such ferocity?

There are a number of factors contributing to heightened ethnic militancy. Some are specific to a region; others are more global or systemic.

A. *A Shift in Priorities.* For 25 years following World War II, much of the world was preoccupied with two fundamental conflicts of global dimensions—the ideologically based East-West conflict between the forces of communism and the forces of democracy and capitalism, and the anticolonial wars of Asia, Africa, and the Middle East. For many ethnic groups in the Third World, nationalist aspirations were forgone for the larger and more immediate task of throwing off the European colonial yoke. While some would contend that economic liberation has not been fully accomplished, from a purely political standpoint, the task is virtually complete. As a result, long-standing ethnic tensions are rising to the surface as repressed minorities assert themselves in an effort to gain autonomy.

B. *Global Economic Integration.* Some of the research into the causes of revolution posits that global economic integration has shifted political activity from the national to the international level and as a result there is a tendency for ethnic minorities within societies to gain state status. As Terry Boswell of Emory University points out, this may have a profound impact on the likelihood for revolutionary activity:

> The result has been a rash of new nation-states and revolutionary groups seeking state power, since only nation-states are legitimate political actors in most international affairs and organizations. The most common example is separatist rebellions by ethnic, tribal or religious subnations. (Boswell, p. 7)

Two additional phenomenon closely related to this perspective include first, the decline in United States hegemony, which has diminished "its ability to prevent or police peripheral rebellions, even among its former client states of Iran, Nicaragua, with the

Philippines and South Korea" (Boswell, p. 7). Second, problems of the 1980s have exacerbated frustrations among both national and subnational groups as they scramble for the division of scarce resources (Simon, p. 92).

C. *The Spread of Democratic Processes.* A wave of democratic movements has swept regions of the world long subject to various forms of authoritarian rule. For the first time in history, every executive in South America has achieved power through open elections. Democratic experiments have swept through Eastern Europe as a result of the collapse of communism. Yet the spread of democratic practices in places such as Eastern Europe and South America carries with it certain risks. One is that democracy is built on pluralism, that is, divergent groups in society articulating and aggregating their interests. In many cases this process facilitates the emergence or reemergence of ethnic group political activity, particularly where minority groups have been repressed or discriminated against. If the democratic process cannot positively respond to ethnic group aspirations, the likelihood of ethnic-based violence is increased.

Of particular note are developments in the Soviet Union. Nowhere is the resurgence of ethnic conflict more evident. As Gail W. Lapidus, director of the Berkeley-Stanford Program in Soviet Studies, points out, there seems little doubt that the reforms of Mikhail Gorbachev have, "unleashed an unprecedented tide of protests and demonstrations across the U.S.S.R. in which national grievances occupy a central place alongside economic unrest" (Lapidus, p. 92). Glasnost and democratic reforms in particular have unleashed long-standing grievances, a phenomenon that the Soviet leadership failed to fully anticipate (Lapidus, pp. 94–95).

Drug Wars

Ethnic wars are certainly not the only form of violent conflict that the world is likely to experience in the next decade. A heightened concern with global drug trafficking may lead to a series of clashes in various parts of the world as major drug-consumer nations like the United States attempt to slow down illegal drug production and distribution, and the governments of drug-producing nation-states like Colombia attempt to regain sovereignty over their own land. Table II lists the primary drug-producing countries and offers us some clues as to the future battlegrounds for these wars.

TABLE II

**MAJOR DRUG-PRODUCING COUNTRIES
ESTIMATED 1988 PRODUCTION IN METRIC TONS**

	Opium	Coca	Marijuana	Hashish
Afghanistan	400–800			200–400
Belize			180	
Bolivia		73,770		
Burma	900–1,200			
Colombia		25,300	1,650	
Ecuador		x-200		
Iran	200–400			
Jamaica			300	
Laos	130–300			
Mexico	30		5,970	
Pakistan	100–200			200
Peru		114,450		
Thailand	35			

Source: Foreign Policy Association, "International Drug Traffic: Unwinnable War?", *Great Decisions 1989*, 1989, pp. 80–81. Data presented adapted from *Cultural Survival Quarterly*, Vol. 9, No. 4: 1985, pp. 6–7.

There seems little question that in this area the United States is taking on what Peter Andreas and Coletta Youngers term the "militarization" of U.S. antidrug efforts (Andreas and Youngers, p. 554). There has been far more emphasis on aggressively moving on the source of illicit drugs as opposed to the consumer side of the equation. The Omnibus Anti Drug Abuse Act of 1988 provided for substantial military assistance to Latin American countries to fight drugs, including $3.5 million in military aid to police forces in South America, waiving the 1974 ban on aid to foreign police forces (Andreas and Youngers, p. 554). The Drug Enforcement Agency has become increasingly paramilitary in its operations within the Andean group of countries.

Aside from questions of efficacy, military and paramilitary antidrug campaigns can have serious long-term political ramifications. In the U.S.-supported effort in Peru, for instance, there has been difficulty determining where the antidrug effort leaves off and the anti-insurgency war against the revolutionary Shining Path begins. What starts out as an antidrug effort might well become full-scale counterinsurgency war.

Classic Aggression

It is difficult to predict the frequency of classic aggression that results from the desire of decisionmakers to simply acquire territory or resources of another country through invasion. Certainly the 2 August 1990 invasion of tiny Kuwait by Iraq demonstrates that the days of the classic aggressor are not over. One hundred and twenty thousand of Saddam Hussein's troops swept into the sheikdom and seized the entire country, and most importantly, the country's oil facilities. This gave Hussein control of approximately 20 percent of the world's oil production.

The invasion was met with a United Nations economic embargo on all trade with Iraq and occupied Kuwait. Various Kuwaiti foreign assets were frozen and an enormous military buildup led by the United States began on the Arabian peninsula and in the Persian Gulf.

Are we likely to see more of this sort of aggression? One might cautiously predict that the probability of classic aggression will increase for two reasons. First, fewer states will be clients of the superpowers. As such they may feel freer to act more independently against their neighbors. Second, as will be noted later in this article, developing countries are becoming less reliant on the superpowers for weapon systems. Many countries in the Third World are involved in not only the buying and selling of arms, but their production as well.

A possible deterrent to classic aggression is swift and unanimous collective action by the international community similar to that which resulted from the Iraqi invasion of Kuwait. There are ample signs that both the United States and the Soviet Union are willing to utilize the collective security procedures of the United Nations for precisely this purpose. How effective a deterrent this kind of action will be is open to question.

Religious Wars

While religion may constitute a basis upon which to define an ethnic minority such as the Sikhs of the Punjab in India, there is a much broader pattern of religious movement which deserves special comment. It is what might be called the transnational holy war or jihad. It is violent conflict conducted on behalf of religious beliefs, perpetrated by religious fanatics who either cross state borders or operate from within societies on behalf of the religion in general. The modern center of concern is with Islamic fundamentalism, which can be found in varying strength across North Africa, the Middle East, South Asia, and Southeast Asia. The movement received an enormous boost in popularity (as well as some practical support), from the 1978-79 Iranian revolution that brought the Ayatollah Khomeini to power. Iran constitutes the only nation-state with an overwhelming majority of Shiite Moslems, the most radical of the Islamic sects. In most other countries they constitute anything from a significant to a minuscule minority. It should, however, be noted that Sunni radicalism surfaced long before the Iranian Revolution of 1978 (Sivan, p. 1). In fact, the 1979 invasion and occupation of the Grand Mosque in Mecca was carried out by radical Sunnis, not Shiites.

The decade of the 1980s witnessed suicide bombings in Lebanon and Kuwait, the assassination of Anwar Sadat in Egypt, the seizure of American and West European hostages in Lebanon, the attacking of the United States Embassy in India, and a host of other violent acts throughout the world of Islam. The 1990s began with Islamic militants making a bloody attempt to seize power in Trinidad and Tobago. Varying degrees of political unrest plagued Jordan, Morocco, Bahrain, Sudan, and Tunisia. Virtually all of these acts were attributed to Moslem radicals and supported the assertion that militant Islam was the wave of the future, that—like dominos—the moderate Sunni governments of the Arab world would fall to legions of violence-prone radicals. A close look at radical Islam in the early 1990s, however, raises doubts as to prospect of increased violence. There are, as pointed out by Dr. Muhammad Shalaan at Al Azher University in Cairo, considerable divisions within the fundamentalist community carried at times to absurd levels (Wright, p. 21). Adeed Dawisha, an Iraqi scholar and presently professor of government and politics at George Mason University, is convinced that "the tide of militant Islamic fundamentalism reached its peak during the three-year period, February 1979–February 1982. Since then, Islamic revolutionary fervor seems to have waned" (Dawisha, p. 139). The primary thinking here is that militant Islamic fundamentalism is failing to expand its political power. It has not replaced any non-fundamentalist government in or out of the Middle East. Additionally, the xenophobic isolation of Iran for the past decade has led it to the brink of economic disaster (Dawisha, p. 139).

Probably the most meaningful indicator that Moslem radicalism had its limits was the behavior of the large Shiite community in Iraq during the Iran-Iraq war. They did not rally to the Iranian side as Teheran had hoped and predicted. There is evidence that nationalism was far more powerful a force for the generation of loyalty than Shiite allegiances. Similarly, as of the time of this writing in February 1991, Iraqi attempts to turn the Persian Gulf war into a holy war against the West did not succeed.

All of this is not to say that the threat of violence perpetrated by elements of Islamic fundamentalism is over. Militant Islam still constitutes a significant threat to the stability of a number of political regimes in and out of the Middle East. Nevertheless, there is very little evidence over the past few years that the world will see a dramatic increase in violence emerging from the radical sects of Islam, particularly in terms of a large-scale jihad.

FUELING THE FIRES OF CONFLICT

While humans can do considerable damage to each other with their hands as well as sticks and stones, modern warfare requires weapons. The reluctance of the superpowers to continue the large-scale funding of guerrilla wars in every corner of the world would seem to be a welcome development. During the 1980s, the share of arms transfers from the United States and the Soviet Union along with France, the United Kingdom, West Germany, and China generally declined (Klare, pp. 146–147). Further, statistics would indicate that the Third World is of decreasing importance in global arms marketing, particularly the importation of weapons. In 1984, the Third World accounted for 67.6 percent of the global total, falling to 66 percent by 1986 and 61.4 percent in 1988. Data like this, however, can be deceiving. With regard to the drop in the share of the arms market of the six traditional major power suppliers, several countries have moved in to take their places—countries like Italy, Czechoslovakia, Spain, Canada, Belgium, the Netherlands, and Sweden. With regard to the Third World position in the arms market, the data can again be deceiving. Over the past three years, the very years of seemingly precipitous decline in share of the market, several European countries—Greece, Spain, and Turkey—all underwent large modernization programs financed by military aid from NATO allies, therefore reducing the percentage share of arms purchasing by the developing states. In addition, 1988 marked the cease-fire between Iran and Iraq, both enormous Third World purchasers of arms (*SIPRI Yearbook 1989*, p. 196).

Third World states themselves are increasingly entering the weapons business, rapidly acquiring the capability to manufacture major weapon systems (ibid., pp. 146–147). Brazil, Chile, China, North Korea, Pakistan, and South Korea, for instance, are all actively pushing their way into the major leagues of weapons development, manufacturing, and sales. Twelve Third World countries now produce combat aircraft, 13 produce trainers and cargo planes, 12 produce major combat vessels, 11 produce armored vehicles of some kind, and 10 produce artillery systems (ibid., p. 145). Perhaps the most striking example is Argentina. Argentina has produced the Condor I, a solid-fuel, single-stage ballistic missile with a range of 100 to 150 kilometers and in a joint venture with Egypt is developing the Condor II with a range of 800 kilometers (ibid., p. 291).

During the decade-long Iran-Iraq war, 41 states sold weapons to either or both belligerents. Of the 41, fully 17 were developing countries—Algeria, Argentina, Brazil, Chile, Egypt, Jordan, Libya, Mexico, North Korea, Pakistan, Philippines, South Korea, Syria, Taiwan, Turkey, and Vietnam (ibid., 1987, pp. 204–205). There seems little doubt that access to the weapons of war will not be a problem for those governments and groups that seek to wage violent conflict.

The harsh reality is that the international arms market is flourishing, Third World nations are increasingly an integral part of that market not only as consumers, but as producers, and the forces of violence in the world will not lack for the weapons of war in the 1990s.

TECHNIQUES OF WAR IN THE 1990s

The vast majority of violent conflicts in the next decade will consist of various forms of urban as well as rural guerrilla warfare in addition to a range of political-military conflict techniques that have been termed low-intensity conflicts. The latter phenomena tend to be less violent than modern conventional warfare and include phenomena such as terrorism and counterterrorism, insurgency and counterinsurgency, and some special operations such as those conducted covertly by various elite military, paramilitary, and intelligence units.* This paper identifies three subjects of particular

---

*For an excellent discussion of the definition of low-intensity conflict, see: Loren B. Thompson, "Low-Intensity Conflict: An Overview," in Loren B. Thompson (ed.), *Low Intensity Conflict: The Pattern of Warfare in the Modern World*, Lexington, Mass.: Lexington Books, 1989, pp. 2-3.

relevance to the issue of technique: the advent of wars without guerrillas, disturbing developments in weapons acquisition, deployment and use in the Third World, and the likelihood of an increase in international terrorism.

Wars Without Guerrillas

Jeffrey D. Simon of the RAND Corporation has recently posited that we are already beginning to experience a sudden, explosive form of revolutionary war that he calls "wars without guerrillas" (Simon, p. 5). Three recent prototypes for this kind of conflict were the people's revolution in the Philippines in 1986, the rioting in Haiti during the same year that forced Jean Claude Duvalier to leave the country, and the intifada on the West Bank and in Gaza in the Middle East. To these examples we might add the revolutions in Eastern Europe during 1989, particularly that which took place in Romania. As Simon notes:

> Revolutions without guerrillas differ in several ways from traditional insurgencies. Whereas it may take a guerrilla army years, or even decades, to overthrow a government or create a sense of crisis throughout a country, political unrest can evolve much more quickly. Governments can be toppled in an matter of weeks, and countries can become paralyzed overnight. (Simon, p. 5)

This vision of rapidly developing, violent, broad-based, spasmodic revolutions on the brink of anarchy has profound policy implications for, among others, major powers like the United States that have defense arrangements, major markets, and other economic interests in the Third World.

Disturbing Weapons Trends

The Iran-Iraq war revealed two very disturbing trends in Third World conflict—the proliferation and use of surface-to-surface missiles, already alluded to in an earlier section of this paper and the use of chemical weapons. As of 1988, no fewer than 20 states of the developing world possessed ballistic missiles with ranges running from 37 to 2,220 kilometers (Karp, p. 14). The introduction of these weapons into crisis areas threatens to alter regional balances of power. They do not require large, elaborate bases, are not as easily intercepted as bombers, and are considerably cheaper to produce and replace than manned aircraft (Karp, p. 14). Finally, as Karp points out, "the most worrisome aspect of Third World ballistic missiles is their potential as nuclear weapons delivery systems" (Karp, p. 14).

The ban on the use of chemical weapons in interstate conflicts is crumbling. Evidence indicates the extensive use of nerve and mustard gas in the Iran-Iraq war and a general proliferation of chemical warfare capabilities in the Third World. At the heart of this development is the increasingly popular perception of the military utility of these weapons ("A Matter of Grave Concern," p. 1). Beyond the United States, Soviet Union, Iran, and Iraq, the press has in recent years reported that many other states are alleged to possess chemical weapons or are suspected of trying to acquire them: Argentina, Chile, Peru, El Salvador, Guatemala, Cuba, Egypt, Syria, Libya, France, Israel, Ethiopia, Angola, South Africa, Burma, Thailand, China, Taiwan, North Korea, South Korea, and Vietnam (Bowman, p. 2).

Terrorism

The 1980s saw significant increases in terrorist activity around the world, particularly between 1983 and 1986 (Hoffman, p. 1). According to the RAND corporation, the six-year period of 1973 to 1979 saw 1,573 terrorist-caused deaths. In the following six years, 1980 to 1986, the number rose to 3,225 (Hoffman, p. 1). Ironically, increased effectiveness in countering terrorism techniques may be partly responsible for this pattern. As security at government installations and on passenger aircraft is enhanced and the techniques for antiterrorist intelligence and hostage-release bargaining have become more effective, terrorists have increasingly resorted to the use of explosives, particularly remote and timed detonations. Put simply, the use of bombs dramatically increases the ability of the terrorist to escape capture or death because there is no necessity for the perpetrator to be near or at the site of destruction.

Another trend in the 1980s was an increase in state-sponsored terrorism. Countries like Iran, Libya, and Syria increasingly utilized terrorism as an instrument of foreign policy (Kidder, p. 13; "More on State Sponsored Terrorism," pp. 1–6). In the 1990s there is likely to be a decline in state-sponsored terrorism as the international community organizes to counter this type of activity and traditional terrorist sponsors like Syria, Iran, and Libya become preoccupied with other issues. Iran in particular is desperate for foreign capital, and its continued support for terrorist activity is an obstacle to the fulfillment of that need.

Although state-sponsored terrorism may decline, widespread frustrations felt by persecuted ethnic minorities referred to earlier in this chapter may lead to a substantial increase in the use of terror tactics both within their societies and internationally. Already, a wide variety of terrorist groups find the motives for their activity deeply rooted in ethnic frustrations and bitterness. Palestinian groups like the Popular Front for the Liberation of Palestine (PFLP), the Popular Front for the Liberation of Palestine-General Command (PFLP-GP) and Abu Nidal are examples, as are the Baathist Saiqa (Storm) out of Syria, the Basque Nation and Liberty (ETA) out of Spain, the Free South Moluccan Organization in the Netherlands, the Armenian Secret Army for the Liberation of Armenia (ASALA) in Turkey, the Indian-based Sendero Luminoso (Shining Path) in Peru, the Kurdish Worker's Party (PKK) in Turkey, and various Indian Sikh groups such as Dashmesh, Dal Khalsa, Babbar Khalsa, and the All India Sikh Students Federation (*Patterns of Global Terrorism: 1987*). It has been said that terrorism is the weapon of the weak. Sometimes it is, and sometimes it is not. It is true that many of the frustrated ethnic minorities suffer from two conditions: first, a desperate need to publicize their cause, and second, the reality that they are in no position to face their governments head-on in any conventional military sense. In fact, they might not be able even to launch a viable guerrilla war. From their perspective, the only viable alternative may be terrorism.

CONCLUSION

The favorable turn in East-West relations, as a result of the rapid delegitimization of European communism, is a welcome event that will no doubt contribute to an easing of international tensions. This development, however, does not mean the end of violent international conflict. This paper has argued first that ethnic and nationalistic tensions are to be found in nearly every part of the world and are likely to spawn considerable violence. Second, there are enormous pressures on high-consumption states to do something about international drug trafficking, and some drug-producing states like Colombia are desperate to regain their own sovereignty from the drug lords who have eroded the state's power to govern itself. Third, there are likely to be some cases of classic aggression unless international collective security measures become a credible deterrent. Fourth, while militant Islam remains a serious concern for the international community, there is doubt as to whether the decade will experience a high-level religious warfare out of the Islamic world. Fifth, regardless of where violence does occur and who is involved, there appears to be no problem with acquiring the weapons of war with the arms trade flourishing in both the northern and southern hemispheres. Finally, three characteristics of violence will be part of the international system of the next decade: first, sudden, large, popularly based, almost spasmodic revolutions, termed wars without guerrillas; the use of chemical weapons and ballistic missiles by Third World countries; and an increase in terrorism as a perceived weapon of necessity by ethnic revolutionaries.

Douglas W. Simon

APPENDIX

ETHNIC/RELIGIOUS GROUPINGS IN EXISTENT OR POTENTIAL VIOLENT TROUBLE SPOTS

The following list consists of ethnic and/or religious groups active in the specified countries. Each group has taken some political action to assert its national identity, ethnic sovereignty, and/or territorial claims to insure its very survival as a distinct culture. In some cases these actions have been within the legal processes of the country. In others, nonviolent acts of defiance have been made. In many cases, violent acts to the point of guerrilla warfare have been undertaken.

The purpose of this list is not to identify specific wars of liberation or to provide a comprehensive list of all ethnic groups in the world (of which this is only a fraction). The purpose is to (A) identify real and potential danger spots where, based on recent history, if violent struggle has not broken out, there exists the potential for such activity; and (B) to emphasize the ethnic complexity of the world as it relates to political violence.

SOUTH ASIA:

India:	Sikhs
Pakistan:	Baluchis
	Paktuns
Sri Lanka:	Tamils
	Sinhalese
Afghanistan:	Pushtuns
	Tajiks
	Uzbeks
	Turkmens
	Hazaras

Iran:	Turkmens Azerbaijani Turks Baluchis Kurds
Bangladesh:	Muslims Buddhists

MIDDLE EAST:

Israel, West Bank, Gaza:	Palestinians Israelis
Egypt:	Shiite Muslims Sunnite Muslims
Turkey:	Armenians Kurds
Lebanon:	Shiite Muslims Sunnite Muslims Maronite Christians Druses Orthodox Greeks Armenian Christians Palestinians

---

EUROPE:

Belgium:	Flemings Walloons
Cyprus:	Greek Cypriots Turkish Cypriots

France:	Basques Corsicans	
Italy:	Sardinians	
Netherlands:	South Moluccans	
Portugal:	Madeirans Azorenes	
Spain:	Basques Madeirans	
U.K.:	Catholics of Northern Ireland	
Yugoslavia:	Croats Serbs Macedonians Montenegrins Slovenes	
U.S.S.R.:	Uzbek: Muslims	Muslims want more political representation in Uzbekistan.
	Tadzhikistan:	Tajiks (Persian) vs. Uzbeks (Turkic). Land dispute.
	Kazakhstan:	(1) 100+ ethnic groups. (2) Ethnic Germans on Russian border.
	Russia:	(1) Mongol Buryats annex two districts outside their small autonomous republic.

(2) Volga Tatars (Muslim) want full republic status and to absorb their fellow Muslims, the Bashkirs.

(3) Karelians. Want to annex all or part of the Kola Peninsula.

(4) Lithuanians

(5) Estonians

(6) Latvians

(7) Konigsberg (Baltic city of Kaliningrad) wants to be designated a separate ethnic group.

(8) Ethnic Poles of southern Lithuania and northwestern Byelorussia want autonomous republic.

(9) Ukrainians

(10) Gagauz (Turkic) Approximately 2,000 want autonomous republic of Moldavia.

(11) Crimean Tatars want Crimean Peninsula back.

(12) Armenians (Christian) vs. Azerbaijani (Muslim) battle over Nagorno-Karabakh.

(13) Ossets of Georgia want to be part of the North Ossetian autonomous republic.

(14) Adzhars secede

from Georgia.
(15) Mesheti Turks want
autonomy.

ASIA AND THE PACIFIC:

China:	Tibetans
Indonesia:	Papuans Timors
Philippines:	Muslim secessionists
Thailand:	Muslim secessionists
Burma:	Karens Kareniri Mons Arakans Chins Kachins Kayahs Shans
New Caledonia:	Melanesians (Kanaks)

NORTH AMERICA:

Canada:	French Canadians
United States:	Native Americans

LATIN AMERICA:

Nicaragua:	Miskito, Sumo, and Ramaquie Indians
Guatemala:	Mayan Indians
Costa Rica:	Boruca
Panama:	Cuna

AFRICA:

Ethiopia:	Tigrayans
	Oromo
	Eritreans
	Bales
	Wollos
Angola:	Ovimbundu
	Bakongo
Nigeria:	Ibo
	Yoruba
	Hausa
	Fulani
Senegal:	Mauritanian herdsman
	Senegalese farmers
Sudan:	Animists
	Christians
	Muslims
	Dinkas
Somalia:	Issaqs
Burundi:	Tutsi
	Hutu

Namibia:	Ovambos
	Hereros
South Africa:	Xhosa
	Zulu
	Afrikaaners
Uganda:	Nilotics
Mozamabique:	Makonde
	Maputo
Chad:	Tubu (Muslim)
	Christian (South)
Zimbabwe:	Shona
	Ndebele

BIBLIOGRAPHY

Andreas, Peter and Youngers, Coletta. "U.S. Drug Policy and the Andean Cocaine Industry." *World Policy Journal*, Summer 1989, pp. 529–562.

Boswell, Terry. "World Revolutions and Revolutions in the World-System." In *Revolution in the World-System*, edited by Boswell. New York: Greenwood Press, 1989.

Bowman, Steven R. "Chemical Weapons: A Summary of Proliferation and Arms Control Activities." CRI Issue Brief, Congressional Research Service, updated 27 March 1989.

David, P. "Between Tribe and State." *Economist* 306 (6 February 1988): 7–8.

Dawisha, Adeed. *The Arab Radicals*. New York: Council on Foreign Relations, 1986.

Douglas, W.A. "A Critique of Recent Trends in the Analysis of Ethnonationalism." *Ethnic Racial Studies*, April 1988, pp. 192–206.

Foreign Policy Association. "International Drug Traffic: Unwinnable War?" *Great Decisions 1989*, pp. 80–81.

Hoffman, Bruce. *The Contrasting Ethical Foundations of Terrorism in the 1980s*. Santa Monica, Calif.: The RAND Corporation, January 1988.

Jansen, G.H. *Militant Islam*. New York: Harper & Row, 1979.

Karp, Aaron. "The Frantic Third World Quest for Ballistic Missiles." *Bulletin of the Atomic Scientists*, June 1988, pp. 14–30.

Kidder, Rushworth. "How Nations Support Terrorist Operations Around the World." *The Christian Science Monitor*, 14 April 1986.

Klare, Michael T. "Deadly Convergence: The Perils of the Arms Trade." *World Policy Journal*, Spring 1989, pp. 141–168.

Lapidus, Gail W. "Gorbachev's Nationalities Problem." *Foreign Affairs*, Fall 1989, pp. 92–108.

Luard, Evan. "War." In *War in International Society*. New Haven: Yale University Press, 1986.

Maffari, Mehdi. "The New Era of Terrorism: Approaches and Typologies." *Cooperation and Conflict: Nordic Journal of International Politics*, 4 November 1989, pp. 179–196.

Merida, Kevin. "Wreckage in Forgotten Lands." *Dallas Morning News*, 6 August 1989, pp. 3M–4M.

"More on State Sponsored Terrorism," *Contemporary Mideast Background*, No. 240 (29 September 1987): 1–6.

Schechterman, Bernard and Slann, Martin, eds. *Violence and Terrorism 90/91*. Annual Editions. Luice Dock, Gulford, Conn.: The Dushkin Publishing Group, Inc., 1990.

Schlagheck, Donna M. *International Terrorism: An Introduction to the Concepts and Actors*. Lexington, Mass.: Lexington Books, 1988.

Segaller, Stephen. *Invisible Armies: Terrorism into the 1990s*. New York: Harcourt, 1986.

Simon, Jeffrey D. *Revolutions Without Guerrillas*. Santa Monica, Ca.: RAND Corporation, 1989.

SIPRI Yearbook 1987, World Armaments and Disarmament. New York: Oxford University Press, 1987.

SIPRI Yearbook 1989, World Armaments and Disarmament. New York: Oxford University Press, 1989.

Sivan, Emmanuel. "Sunni Radicals in the Middle East and the Iranian Revolution." *International Journal of Middle East Studies,* (February 1989): 1–30.

Small, Melvin and Singer, J. David. *Resort to Arms: International and Civil Wars 1816–1980.* Beverly Hills, Ca.: Sage Publications, 1982.

__________. *International War: An Anthology.* 2d ed. Chicago: The Dorsey Press, 1984.

Thompson, Loren B. *Low Intensity Conflict: The Pattern of Warfare in the Modern World.* Lexington, Mass.: Lexington Books, 1989.

United States Department of State. *Patterns of Global Terrorism: 1987.* Department of State Publication 9661, August 1988.

United States Arms Control and Disarmament Agency. "A Matter of Grave Concern: Chemical Weapons: Putting the Genie Back in the Bottle." *Arms Control Update.* October 1988.

United States Senate. Committee on Foreign Relations and the Committee on the Judiciary. *International Terrorism, Insurgency and Drug Trafficking: Present Trends in Terrorist Activity.* Washington, D.C.: 99th Congress, 1st Session, Senate Hearing 99–372 (SD Cat. no. Y 4.J 89/2:S. hrg. 99–372), 13-15 May 1985.

Wright, Robin. "Holy Wars: The Ominous Side of Religion in Politics." *The Christian Science Monitor,* 12 November 1987, pp. 20–21.

CHAPTER FIVE

International Economics in the 1990s: Systems in Transition

VIVIAN A. BULL

INTRODUCTION

The international economic system that emerged following World War II and remained basically intact for 45 years is undergoing dramatic changes. The system is no longer dominated by the hegemonic power of the United States. New economic and political alignments are being formed, the most visible of which is the European Community (EC), an organization of 12 nations committed to completing an integrated internal market by 1992. The impact of this movement will be to establish three economic powers, the United States, Japan, and the European Community. This change will also significantly affect those nations which are not a part of this triad. Nations surrounding the EC may seek special relationships with the EC, as will those nations with historic economic relations with individual European countries. As the economic power shifts to an East-West axis, serious questions must be raised about the well-being of those nations south of the triad powers.

As if these concerns and transitions were not complicated enough, the revolutions of 1989 opened up the nations of Eastern Europe to new economic and political systems, all of which will have an impact upon developing relationships within the world economic order. The Gulf War, being fought at this time, has already created large dislocations of workers, reduced or eliminated remittances of the guest workers to home countries, and has realigned the traditional political and economic relationships in the Middle East. The full economic impact of the war is only now coming under consideration and it is yet to be measured in either human, political, or economic costs. In another part of the world, the newly industrialized countries of the Pacific Rim have grown rapidly, but are reaching a stage in their development of slower growth, with fewer opportunities for other nations to follow their pattern of success.

International economic relationships among nations are often defined in terms of trade and aid. Traditional relationships here are undergoing change, as well. We have relied upon the General Agreement on Tariffs and Trade (GATT) to "regulate" international trade. Issues of self-interest and national protection may create barriers to freer trade for what may be an advantage in the world marketplace may create disadvantages in the domestic market. Developing nations are voicing more articulately their needs and concerns, and the world community must be aware of the need for increased responsibility in terms of improving economic conditions for those in the developing world, as well as for those in the newly emerging states of Eastern Europe.

A new global understanding of the economic order goes beyond political/economic alignments and trade relations. Corporate entities which have become international may operate with an impact similar to that of a traditional nation-state. Globalization must also address problems of world order. Moreover, such issues as population growth, debt repayment, exchange rate mechanisms, and financial market interdependencies will be of increasing importance in the future.

This essay will examine the major issues facing the international economic order in the 1990s and beyond by focusing on three major trends: economic integration, improving trade relations, and globalization. The emphasis will not be upon the problems of change, but rather upon the new possibilities and the potential benefits which may come from the changing world economic order. The dramatic changes going on in the realm of international economics hold out the possibility of greater world prosperity, but there are also a number of problems which must be carefully managed to reach that greater prosperity.

THE MOVEMENT TOWARD GREATER ECONOMIC INTEGRATION

Since 1985 the European Community has been dominated by the conflict of ideas and possibilities over the implementation of the Single European Act which set into motion the completion of the internal market, scheduled for 1992. New economic relationships are being created within a more integrated European Community and these new relationships will also have considerable impact as well upon the world community of nations. This plan for a Europe without frontiers has been implemented because of a number of circumstances coming together at a particular time in history. Leading EC officials were determined to reinvigorate the Community and attempt to fulfill the promise of the Treaty of Rome by taking the EC further towards union. Leading European industrialists were concerned about remaining in competition with the increasing economic strength of the other members of the "triad," the United States and Japan. National leaders within the Community were desiring an economic strategy which would guarantee growth and employment within an expanded economic environment, one which would be larger than any nation-state could provide. It is probable that no one of these factors would have changed the course of the EC by itself, but the confluence of these interests has added up to a potential economic revolution (Owen and Dynes, p. 8).

The problems associated with 1992 have not been small, nor will all the resolutions and activities actually be completed by 1992; but the program has begun and it now carries a certain momentum which cannot be stopped, though there may be changes in its course. Countries and leaders continue to try to influence the Community's activities, sometimes with self-interest in mind, but the will of the Community is moving on to 1992. The programs will continue after 1992 and it is probable that the European Court will have to deal with continuing disputes over the 1992 directives. It appears certain that the European Community is acquiring a say in many of the issues that were once regarded as the exclusive preserve of national governments.

The year 1992 is a complex of directives, regulations, and other measures which, when added together, create a distinct change in the way the European Community is organized and the way it is governed. In reality, 1992 is developing beyond the confines of the original White Paper which outlined the plan in 1985. It is taking on a life of its own, for almost any European-wide initiative can now be related to 1992. Though 1992 currently deals with economic integration, there are many who envision political integration as another step in the process, just as there are those who strongly oppose further political integration.

The major impacts of the completion of the internal market on the way people live and do business will include the following:

1. **A large open market:** 338 million customers (including those of united Germany) await the efforts of EC and foreign businesses, with all firms competing on equal terms in a huge open market. Public authorities must give enterprises from any EC nation an equal opportunity to win high-value contracts.

2. **Cross-border savings:** Frontier delays of delivery trucks and complicated customs procedures cost an estimated $27 billion according to the European Parliament. Simplified customs procedures will save many of these costs.

3. **Easier travel:** Controls will be abolished at the EC's internal frontiers, although not at its external points of entry. Single-format EC passports will cut down delays.

4. **Professional qualifications:** There will be universal recognition of qualifications and diplomas, though linguistic barriers may still cause problems.

5. **Consumer protection:** Broad criteria and common standards are being developed regarding labelling, health, and safety standards.

6.   **Free competition:** Protectionist practices preventing free competition will be illegal. More liberal policies have already been introduced in the aviation and trucking industries.

7.   **Harmonization of value-added and indirect taxes:** Similar tax structures will eliminate distortions to trade resulting from large differences in tax rates among the countries.

8.   **Harmonization of technical standards:** Common standards will be established in the television and broadcasting industries as well as in telecommunications.

9.   **Financial services:** The EC will remove all restrictions on capital movements and will harmonize standards for prudent supervision and protection of investors. There will be expanded use of the European Currency Unit (ECU), and there is some discussion of establishing a European Central Bank. Monetary issues are in the early stages of discussion and negotiation.

(See Owen and Dynes, pp. 20–21.)

Just as the Community was becoming comfortable with its internal process, having passed about one-third of the required directives for completing the internal market, the European scene began to change. In the late summer of 1989, the barbed wire fence was cut on the Hungarian border and East Germans began to flow out through the broken fence heading for West Germany. What followed could not have been predicted, from the breach in the wall to the overthrow of long-standing, all powerful, and controlling Communist regimes. The cry for freedom rang out and was answered. But the euphoria of the hours and days of change was soon to be tempered by the reality of the understanding of the economic impact of freedom and reform. Just as the Marshall Plan is credited with having provided a basis which allowed the European countries to begin recovery and which led to the Treaty of Rome, so now again there was a need for a similar organization. Plans for the European Bank for Reconstruction and Development are being laid. There is an interesting "sign-of-the-times" element here, for the bank will be denominated in EC's rather than in dollars as has traditionally been the case in world economic organizations. It has taken Americans some time to adjust to the fact that their request is being met; that is, the EC is assuming a larger share of its global responsibilities, even in the currency arena.

In May 1990, the EC Commission developed a plan that would allow the world's richest industrialized countries to help Bulgaria, East Germany, Czechoslovakia, Yugoslavia, and Romania switch to market-oriented economies. The EC assumed responsibility for coordinating assistance offered in cash and kind by 24 nations which had agreed originally to help Poland and Hungary and which then extended the assistance to the above nations. Ministers of the Group of 24 provided approval of the extended plan. All five countries want better access to EC markets, and each country also presented a list of priorities which included industrial restructuring, investment in transport and telecommunications, training, and development of tourism, among other requests. The EC Commission's statement listed environmental protection as a high priority for all five countries. This is an example of the increasing interdependence among nations which only recently had few or modest economic relations. These trends are important. They point toward the possibility of greater prosperity through broader European economic integration. They are also significant because they point toward greater East-West security. In this context it would be interesting to explore the following question: If Western European economic integration has been successful in overcoming German-French rivalry (as illustrated by World Wars I and II), will wider European economic integration (including Eastern nations and the U.S.S.R.) overcome Western-Soviet political rivalry?

The estimates of the costs associated with rebuilding the infrastructure and converting the Eastern European economies vary greatly, but they are all of a very large magnitude. As more economic information is collected, it has become obvious that the costs associated with cleaning up the environment alone will be enormous. There is a need to develop massive aid programs, joint venture opportunities for private investment, credit arrangements—

all manner of support for resource and technological development. Early efforts have been significant but modest in terms of long-run needs. As these nations are brought into the world trading sphere, as their currencies become convertible, and as their people begin to participate in the world marketplace, the potential for world economic growth is considerable. There is a fear, however, among the developing nations, that as concern for aid and assistance shifts to the nations of Eastern Europe whose needs are so great, that the resources available to nations in need in other parts of the world will diminish. The response to the calls and needs for economic assistance from all developing nations will require a major commitment on behalf of the developed economies into the 1990s and beyond.

As the world watches, the political changes in Europe continue; the changes will have varying effects upon traditional economic relationships and new structures will be developed. As the world becomes more interdependent, it also becomes more complex, and there will be an increasing need for collective decision making through multilateral diplomacy. Economic negotiators will need flexibility as never before, not only to respond to changing conditions, but to anticipate and provide direction for a new economic environment. International institutions—such as the U.N., the European Court, and GATT—will take on a greater importance as forums for negotiation and settlements.

THE MOVEMENT TOWARD FREER TRADE

Today's world trading relationships are dominated by the European Community, the United States, and Japan. This triad represents roughly 58 percent of world trade and nearly two-thirds of the global gross national product. The global level of imports and exports has grown rapidly in the last ten years, and this expansion of trade has contributed significantly to a decade of mostly uninterrupted growth in the industrial nations. The organization which has facilitated this expansion is the General Agreement on Tariffs and Trade (GATT). Founded in 1948, GATT is a legal and institutional framework consisting of agreed multilateral trade rules, procedures for trade liberalization, and a mechanism for dispute settlement.

At GATT's founding, the United States and 22 other countries met to cut tariff rates for industrial goods. In the early years, the tariff reductions were modest and primarily geared toward rebuilding the war-torn European economies. In the 1960s North-South economic relations became an increasingly important issue. By then GATT was dominated by developing countries, which constituted two-thirds of its membership. They continued to demand more consideration for their own economic trade needs, and as they had not yet achieved a strong export position, that was granted. Relationships among the GATT members have survived some difficult times, including periods of protectionism and increasing levels of economic development; however, on many issues agreement has not been reached. In 1986, the Uruguay Round of discussions was designed to create a new framework for continued formal negotiations. Though there are still issues of contention, recently there has been a greater willingness of GATT members to refrain from new protective measures and to resort to GATT procedures for resolving bilateral trade conflicts (see Fleiss, pp. 13–14). Most of the differences among the members of GATT are industry-specific or trade issues in agriculture, automobiles, computer software, and aviation products, to mention a few. Most nations seemed to be committed to achieving success in the Uruguay Round of GATT talks, which were scheduled to conclude in December 1990. Unfortunately, negotiations were suspended in December when it became apparent that there was to be no resolution of the dispute involving agriculture, more particularly the large subsidies which the EC provides for its farmers. The negotiators did return to Geneva in late January 1991 and talks are to continue, though it is difficult to forecast their outcome.

Within GATT, the triad nations appear to be in general agreement on the need for liberalizing services and removing trade-related investment restrictions. There is agreement on a need to extend national treatment to banks, insurance companies, law firms, and other service-related firms and to provide free market access, providing such access does not violate existing national regulations. Most support the removal of restrictions on local equity holdings, repatriation of profits, and produce mandate requirements. The issue of tariffs on textiles continues to be complicated, for textiles are important to the EC and to the United States, both of which have strong lobby groups. However, textiles are also important to many developing nations whose interests are often not so clearly represented in the negotiations. These developing nations continue to point out that the industrialized nations are more interested in efforts to liberalize areas of investment, services, and intellectual property protection, than in attending to issues of importance to the poor countries, issues such as textiles, safeguards, tropical products, dumping and subsidies (see Rockwell, pp. 7–8).

The agriculture problem will continue to be at the center of any discussions. Each of the triad powers has a special interest in protecting its own agriculture industry; each is concerned about protecting the small farmer. At the midterm Uruguay Round meeting in Montreal in December 1988, agricultural exporters from the developing nations, including Argentina, Brazil, and Chile, said they would abandon support for the talks unless significant reforms were made in the U.S. and EC farm policies. Agricultural policies were a focus of the discussions of the heads of state of the G-7 nations (Canada, France, Germany, Italy, Japan, United Kingdom, United States) in July 1990 in Houston, but little progress was made, and the issue was left unresolved. The United States argued for improved market access, an end to export subsidies, and the gradual elimination of domestic support for farm production. The United States supports eliminating import quotas on farm products in favor of tariffs. The EC and Japan reject this position, arguing that it would not enable the countries to manage cyclical crises brought on by weather or market conditions. Brussels has proposed to progressively reduce production payments and market support systems, but has provided no time table. Each of the triad has very restrictive policies which each defends vigorously. The result of these policies is not only higher food prices to the consumers, but also some degree of stability for the farmers (see Rockwell, pp. 8–9).

In late July 1990, the United States and the EC suspended negotiations for a month, as they failed to make progress in resolving the trade dispute over farm subsidies. This delay caused considerable concern, for the deadline for the conclusion of the

Uruguay Round negotiations, December 1990, was not far away. It is estimated that half of the nations in the GATT trade talks have indicated that they would "walk away from negotiations if Washington and Brussels cannot agree on measures to end protectionism in agricultural trade" (C. Farnsworth, *New York Times*, 25 July 1990). As a matter of fact, negotiations were suspended but later resumed. Many analysts fear that failure of the Uruguay Round could result in protectionist trading blocs that could hamper global prosperity. Timely action by those committed to successful completion of the Uruguay Round became extremely important.

Though many of these GATT issues appear to divide the nations into industrialized and developing nation groups, there has been a consistent commitment to GATT and its procedures as being important for world trade. As nation-states become a part of larger trading units, issues of nationalistic protection should become less important and issues which can provide regional benefits may be more important. Short-term economic costs will need to be balanced by widespread longer-term economic benefits.

It will be necessary in the years ahead to guard against the possibility of the special interests of the triad powers becoming dominant in international relations. Greater emphasis will need to be placed on improving the wealth and welfare of the global community, for otherwise the increasing strength within the triad sector will completely overwhelm those nations and peoples outside of the triad. In June 1990, prior to the meeting of the industrialized G-7 nations, there was another economic summit. In Kuala Lumpur, Malaysia, the first meeting of the "Group of Fifteen" nations was convened. The members include Algeria, Argentina, Brazil, Egypt, India, Indonesia, Jamaica, Malaysia, Mexico, Nigeria, Peru, Senegal, Venezuela, Yugoslavia, and Zimbabwe. The combined populations of the G-15 nations total 29.6 percent of the world's population, whereas the populations of the G-7 nations total 12.7 percent. The summit's final communique included references to a new post–Cold War global economy and a need for North-South sharing of responsibility. These concerns need more specific definition in order for the developed world to respond adequately. Key issues of concern include unresolved external debt problems and the ongoing transfer of resources from poor to rich nations. The G-15 have pledged to continue to meet and form common approaches to their economic problems. They also reaffirmed a commitment to "a balanced and successful conclusion to the Uruguay Round of GATT negotiations which takes into account the concerns and needs of developing nations" (H. Henderson, *CSM*, 9 July 1990). For many of these nations, the end of the Cold War frees the societies to explore alternate paths which may lie between strict capitalist or socialist development (as in Zimbabwe). The 1990s are likely to generate complex new development models, and the G-15 nations will have much to contribute to the discussions.

The possibility of GATT being strengthened must also be considered. Interest must be directed toward managing trade in services, establishing rules for international investment, and looking after exchanges of intellectual property such as patents and copyrights. This would enlarge the scope of the Uruguay Round considerably. The changing political atmosphere may actually be offering some hope for success, for the Eastern European nations appear to be genuinely intent upon joining the Western economic and trading system. Whereas the old regimes did not want to open up their economies to world commerce, the new governments regard GATT trade rules as a lever for pushing difficult economic reforms at home. The Soviet Union has been granted observer status at GATT and was planning economic reforms that might eventually make its full membership possible. Some developing countries are liberalizing their economies, abolishing some controls on trade, and reforming exchange rates. This may allow for greater participation of all members in future rounds of negotiations. These changes in attitude and activity have given GATT a higher priority in the minds of Western leaders, and this may contribute to a deeper commitment to achieving success in future rounds of negotiations.

While the larger group discussions are taking place, there are also discussions among smaller trading groups. The seven-member European Free Trade Association (EFTA) which includes Finland, Norway, Sweden, Iceland, Switzerland, and Austria, has been in discussion with the 12-nation European Community. The combination of these two groups would create a virtually borderless European market extending from Finland to Spain and including more than 360 million consumers. It has been proposed that much of the EC's single market be extended to include the EFTA nations, and negotiations are going forward, but not as rapidly as expected. The two organizations want to create a European Economic Space (EES)—a proposed free trade and free circulation zone that would constitute the world's largest and wealthiest market. The aims are twofold: (1) to extend as far as possible to EFTA nations the free movement of goods, services, capital, and people that the EC aims to achieve by the end of 1992; and (2) to step up cooperation in other areas such as social welfare, environmental protection, and research and development. There are important reasons for these negotiations to succeed. The EC has more trade with the EFTA nations than with the United States and Japan combined (H. LaFranchi, *CSM*, 18 May 1990). The EC also hopes that including the EFTA nations in a trading relationship might slow down the number of applicants for EC membership. With a decrease in East-West tensions and more discussions of European-wide security measures, some of the political obstacles that have discouraged EFTA's neutral countries from seeking membership may be removed. The EFTA nations are also concerned that they be included in the new single market, with its important economic benefits. The key problem facing the negotiators is determining how much influence EFTA should have in shaping and making EC decisions.

It is yet to be determined what the impact of the opening of the Eastern European economies will mean for intra-European and global trading relationships. In the early stages of development there is a great need for loans and credits to encourage Western corporate investments and to finance major public works to reconstruct the infrastructure. Much of this assistance will be directed through the European Bank for Reconstruction and Development (EBRD), a new multilateral lending institution founded in response to the east central European nations' revolutions in 1989. The EBRD will have a capital base of $12 billion, with some 40 capital donors. The United States, the largest shareholder, will contribute 10 percent. This effort has been compared to the Marshall Plan which contributed so significantly to the reconstruction of Western Europe after World War II. Though of similar intent, EBRD is more modest in scale than the Marshall Plan. EBRD will also be working with a larger number of nations, which have much greater needs in terms of current day development.

Since the early days of the Cold War, the United States and 16 other Western countries have been members of the Coordinating Committee on Multilateral Export Controls, or Cocom. Political changes in Eastern Europe and the virtual disappearance of the Warsaw Pact have led Cocom to revamp its policies, reducing its controls on high technology exports. This has been a most dramatic change in the guidelines for an organization which was established in 1949 to prevent Western technology from being used for military purposes by the Soviet bloc. Cocom controls are being rewritten to reduce the number of controlled items, to make the list easier to enforce, and to tighten restrictions on exports of specific "truly sensitive items." Preferential treatment will be given to Eastern Europe in the early stages, particularly to Poland, Hungary, and Czechoslovakia. It should be noted that there is no longer total agreement as to the necessity of continuing the work of Cocom.

There has been much discussion about the "peace dividend" in the press if not in economic circles. This gain in budgetary reserves should result from decreased military expenditures as a result of the new era of cooperation between East and West and the decline of the Cold War confrontational atmosphere. Many economists feel that this dividend is illusory. The Iraqi invasion of Kuwait in August 1990 underscored the illusory character of the peace dividend, and the outbreak of war in January 1991 saw the dividend disappear. It is unlikely that there will be any surpluses available in national budgets, and the world's humanitarian problems are increasing as the war continues. The resources that could have addressed the world problems of poverty, disease, and homelessness, to name a few, will need to be generated as a result of a greater commitment to establishing these problems as priority issues in world aid projects.

Although more interest has been focused on developing relations within the East-West axis, new programs directed to the South are being undertaken. In July 1990 President Bush sought to reassure the nations of the southern hemisphere by announcing an enterprise program for the Americas. The Bush plan initially deals with the official debt owed to the U.S. government. Some countries may see 50 percent of their obligation written off, with relief to be negotiated on $7 billion in U.S. government credits and aid. The new plan goes beyond the debt issue and proposes a hemisphere-wide free-trade zone based on agreements similar to the pact the United States has with Canada. The dream is that after years of negotiations, goods would flow between the hemispheres without barriers. Because some countries are not ready to move to free trade, the proposal would be incremental in implementation and may take from five to 15 years for completion. The proposal would also establish a $300 million annual investment fund to advance economic reform in Latin America, with funds coming from the United States, the EC, and Japan. Economists agree that the proposal has tremendous economic potential for the region (see Scherer, p. 4).

There is also a North-South initiative developing in the EC. In the summer of 1990, officials from Spain, France, Italy, and Portugal began organizing a major international initiative to encourage political stability and economic development in the Mediterranean region. There is an element of acknowledged self-interest as the countries fear a surge of Islamic fundamentalism and deepening poverty which could bring a new wave of Muslim immigrants to the EC countries. But they also argue that with the collapse of Communism in Eastern Europe and the disintegration of the Warsaw Pact, the southern rim of the Mediterranean could emerge as the greatest single threat to Western Europe's security . . . being used here "in the broadest of senses, from migratory flows to food supplies" (A. Riding, *NYT*, 30 July 1990). The proposal is to hold a conference on security and cooperation in the Mediterranean, modeled after the 35-nation Conference on Security and Cooperation in Europe. The CSCE has served as a forum for East-West negotiations for the last 15 years. The four EC countries have established working relations with Morocco, Algeria, Tunisia, Libya, and Mauritania. These nations are members of the Arab Maghreb Union which is also discussing the idea of forming a common market among themselves. Eventually more countries from the Mediterranean and from Europe will be involved. The plan would establish an informal forum for regional cooperation in the Mediterranean, and as with the CSCE, it calls for three separate topic areas to be identified: economic cooperation, security, and the human dimension. The intent is to have a "global approach to the region's problems, incorporating everything from population growth and urban concentration to Islamic fundamentalism, unemployment, and immigration" (A. Riding, *NYT*, 30 July 1990). It should be noted that, in recognition of the increasing needs of North Africa, the director of Mediterranean Policy at the European Commission has recently proposed a $3.3 billion package of assistance for eight countries of the region. This is to suggest that there is a growing awareness of the economic issues being greater than those currently dominant in traditional East-West relationships.

This concern for a more global attitude was underscored in August 1990, when Iraq invaded and then annexed Kuwait. President Saddam Hussein thus controlled approximately 20 percent of the world's oil supply. There was a fear that he would also invade Saudi Arabia, and if he were successful, he would then control approximately 40 percent of the world's oil supply. Clearly, this would be an unacceptable condition in the world market. In January 1991 the coalition forces went to war against Iraq, and the geopolitical and economic discussions are again dominated by natural resources issues: Where are the resources and who controls them? The industrialized nations are particularly vulnerable to resource price shocks, as seen in the oil crisis of the 1970s and more recently, during the Iraq-Kuwait dispute. When oil prices are low there is little need to develop alternative sources of energy, but high prices stimulate exploration and research for alternate sources. Diversification may actually alleviate some vulnerability within the economic system.

Another group of nations that must be examined in any contemporary discussion of international economics are the newly industrialized countries, or NICs. This group includes Brazil, Hong Kong, Mexico, Singapore, South Korea, and Taiwan. The NICs burst into the world manufacturing markets late in the 1960s and in the early 1970s. By 1978, these six and India accounted for 70 percent of the developing world's manufactured products (Broad, p. 81). Several other countries have tried to join this group, but it appears that only Malaysia and Thailand will make it. There are a number of reasons why further rapid development of the NICs may not be possible in today's economy. There have been far-reaching changes in the global economy with many national efforts to provide domestic substitutes for goods which had been imported. Some countries have attempted industrialization and have incurred unsustainable levels of external debt. The stronger international economy also makes it more difficult for new entrants. An OECD study has found that the NICs have gradually been losing their comparative advantage as Western industries, such as textiles and electronics, which had located in the NICs for cost reasons, are beginning to move back home because of cost saving innovations in production technology and rising labor costs in the NICs. Other companies have moved to establish residency in locations which will be significant after 1992 and in relation to the U.S.–Canada Free Trade Agreement; that is, they have moved to set up plants within the EC or within the U.S.–Canada free-trade area, in order to gain a trading advantage (Rowley, p. 79).

There is a great concern about the future of the NICs. It is probable that their growth will continue, but growth rates of the past will not be achieved. The OECD study suggests that NICs need to work for greater absorption of production in their domestic markets. The prime minister of Malaysia has declared that "Malaysia does not intend to become a NIC. Happiness is more important than an economic status symbol" (Balakrishnan, p. 96). Malaysia sees the designation as a mixed blessing, for once it has been so designated, the country will lose reduced tariff privileges offered under the generalized system of preferences which have been significant in the Malaysian economy in the past. In the early 1980s Malaysia did introduce an import substitution program, producing domestic goods to replace imports, but it met with mixed results. She has also launched a New Economic Policy program, parts of which, such as the ethnic employment quotas, are irritating to the multinational companies. The OECD study suggested that the NICs should not tie their currencies so closely to the dollar. These countries were severely affected by the economic downturn in the United States in the early 1980s. The NICs need to diversify their markets as well as to increase value added in manufacturing if they are to avoid future economic problems. The World Bank, a proponent of moving countries up the NIC ladder, introduced structural adjustment loans which were dependent upon economic reforms in the recipient country. The World Bank has developed a broad set of policy prescriptions that are designed to improve efficiency in economic sectors which are oriented towards producing exports. This policy orientation is being called into question, given the experiences of the NICs in recent years. There has been a concern that the "debate on adjustment and development should be reopened; strategies that proclaim that the only option is greater dependence on an increasingly hostile and turbulent world economy need to be challenged" (Broad, p. 103). The future of the NICs will be closely related to the changing world economic environment. It is less likely that newly industrializing countries will be able to achieve the high growth rates of the original NIC nations, or that even the original NICs will be able to sustain high growth rates in the future.

The discussion on trade began with a description of the General Agreement on Tariffs and Trade and the ramifications of the major difficult issues in the continuing round of negotiations. The full impact of the Gulf War will need to be evaluated in terms of overall impact on the world economy. But trade issues lie at the core of development and growth, not only for the industrialized nations, but also for the newly industrializing and developing nations. As the world economy becomes "smaller" and more economically interdependent, the issues become both more important and more complex.

THE MOVEMENT TOWARD GLOBALIZATION

Globalization will be the basis for much of business in the 1990s. Companies are becoming truly international, as opposed to multinational. In the past, large firms treated foreign operations as distant appendages for producing products designed and engineered at home. The chain of command and the nationality of the company were clear. Today, no single country dominates the world economy or holds a monopoly on innovation, new technology, capital, or talent. The most sophisticated manufacturing companies are doing research in foreign labs, selling shares to foreign investors, developing an international team of leaders and managers. A series of mergers and acquisitions in recent years has further changed the concept of national control. Social, political, and cultural differences are now incorporated into the culture and ethos of the organization, rather than being ignored.

In the mid-1980s Japan had become the largest source of direct foreign investment, replacing the United States in that position. During the 1980s there was a great expansion of European firms both through investment and by acquisition. During this time U.S. firms tended to concentrate on domestic development. But with the coming of 1992, there has been a great increase in investment and joint-venture activity by foreign forms within the EC.

Corporations are finding a number of advantages in their new international guise. Trade restrictions can be overcome with production facilities located in areas not restricted by domestic policy. Some European firms find the political environment in the United States more conducive to supporting research, because controversies regarding safety and the environment, for instance, have already been resolved. Some companies have expanded to sidestep regulatory hurdles and achieve certain gains due to differentials in labor markets.

Though most governments want to regulate world corporations better, they also find themselves competing to capture some of the more than $150 billion a year that corporations invest across national borders (*Business Week*, 14 May 1990, p. 105). World companies choose countries with the most hospitable atmosphere and the best educated labor force, or perhaps the cheapest labor force. Although governments are fully sovereign within their own borders, or within the borders of the EC, stateless corporations may try to influence policy by offering technology, jobs, and capital. Host governments and nations must learn to negotiate while creating a climate so that the benefits of globalization may be shared by all participants.

To this point the discussion, although it has noted some potential dangers, has focused mainly upon many of the positive changes which will enhance international economic relationships. There are, however, a number of serious problems which the world will face, all of which may have a dampening impact upon future development. To focus on population and financial issues is not to suggest that they are the only issues of concern, but rather that they may have the largest impact on economic development and trade in the 1990s and beyond.

Vivian A. Bull

POPULATION

When Jean-Claude Paye, head of the Organization for Economic Cooperation and Development, a group of 24 industrialized nations, was asked what worried him most on the horizon, he responded: "It depends if you talk short-term or long-term. The serious [long-term] concern . . . is demography. Third World countries are building up population at a rate no imaginable economic development effort could accommodate" (F. Lewis, *NYT*, 14 July 1990). Over the past 30 years, the world's population has grown at a tremendous rate, from three billion in 1960 to more than five billion today. The United Nations projections suggest that the world population will reach six billion by 1999, and in 2010, it will exceed seven billion (U.N., *World Populations: Trends and Policies*).

The rate of population growth varies among countries and regions. While world population was estimated to be increasing at a rate of 1.63 percent a year in 1985–90, the rate was highest in Africa (3 percent) and lowest in the developed countries (0.6 percent). In 1985, half the world's population was under 23.5 years of age, but the median age for the world is expected to rise to 26.5 in 2000 and to 31.2 years in 2025. Thus the dependency ratio will decline, but there will also be increased demand for employment. It is probable that the ratio will increase slowly in developed regions and will decline in developing regions, providing employment is available (Hine, p. 4).

Along with the increase in population has been an increasing trend towards urbanization of the world's population. In 1985, 40 percent of the population were urban residents. This ratio is expected to rise to 50 percent by 2010 (U.N. data). Increasingly the same tendency is found not only in industrialized countries, but in developing countries also as people move to urban areas in search of employment. The concern is whether adequate preparation is being made to absorb these movements and to prepare the economies of the countries to cope with both increasing populations and changing rural/urban patterns of living.

The impression is often given that industrialized countries are turning more and more into service economies, thus diminishing their traditional role as producers of economic goods. The term services includes a wide variety of activities, from investment banking to social and personal services. While some market services cater to personal consumption, many are linked to the production of goods. As companies have downsized, more work has been contracted to outside vendors, thus increasing the demand for services externally. For the OECD countries as a group, services directly linked to goods production accounted for only 25 percent of total value added (OECD, *Development Cooperation: 1988 Report*). So production of goods and services accounted for approximately two-thirds of all gross national product. However, services have continued to grow in importance, and for some developed countries, services sector income is an important part of total trading activity. For instance, the U.K. is both a financial center and a major international creditor, while Austria depends upon tourism for revenue flows. The balance between industrialization and the services sector will become more important as developing and developed nations work more closely in an integrated world economy. An understanding of these sector changes must be incorporated in the development plans of both countries and regional organizations.

FINANCIAL ISSUES

There are a number of issues that fall under this general category. Foremost under consideration in early 1991 is the cost of the war effort in the Gulf and the reconstruction and rehabilitation needs which will have to be met at the conclusion of the fighting. Just as there is some cost sharing to support the armed conflict, there will have to be burden sharing for the reconstruction of the physical and economic conditions in many countries which have been severely affected.

In the early 1980s many developing countries began to experience great difficulty in servicing their debt, that is in paying the interest, much less the principal, on outstanding debt. More recently, through restructuring and implementation of adjustment programs, the situation in some countries has improved, most notably in Mexico and Chile. There is, however, a growing sense of frustration and an increasing cost associated with managing heavy debt burdens. Various programs have been proposed, and for a number of reasons there has been little success. Sometimes adjustment efforts are relaxed too quickly; sometimes there are difficulties in developing markets which may be dominated by industrialized nations; sometimes committed financial support has not materialized. The Brady initiative introduced by U.S. Secretary of the Treasury Nicholas Brady in 1989 sought to bring debtors and creditors together to manage the issues involved. The plan supported the idea that each country was different and the problems of each must be dealt with separately, and that domestic structural reform was a precondition for economic recovery. The debt issue will dominate relations between debtors and creditors, for it is an issue of immense importance.

Financial flows to developing countries come primarily from governments and international institutions. Lending from the private sector has been weak since the middle 1980s, a direct reflection of the debt crisis. The United Nations has set a target rate of 0.7 percent of GNP to be paid out as an Official Development Assistance payment. In order for the donor country's payment to qualify as an Official Development Assistance payment, more than 25 percent of the payment must be directly related to the recipient country's economic development (Hein, p. 20). Were the U.N. target level to be achieved by all industrialized nations, it could have an enormous positive impact on the aid flows to developing nations. Each year the Development Assistance Committee (DAC), an official OECD forum of 18 major donor countries, publishes comparative data showing which members exceed or fall short of the 0.7 percent target. Though some members have consistently exceeded the target, the overall ratio in both nominal and real terms has remained relatively low, not exceeding 0.4 percent. DAC foresees a number of trends for the 1990s:

1. Developing countries are likely to seek more direct assistance for their private sectors.

2.   Financial flows from private sources will gradually turn around from their present low levels, a process that has already begun in Asia.

3.   Donors will continue to give highest priority to the lowest income countries.

4.   Donors may well rethink and revise their aid policy for the so-called upper-middle-income countries that are likely to move into the ranks of the newly industrializing countries.

(DAC, as quoted in Hine, p. 20.)

These trends point up the need for increased support from the private sector, that is from private investors. This would also suggest a tendency for nations to want to support the most needy countries, rather than to continue support to those nations who may be developing into strong competitors in the international marketplace. Aid may increasingly be used to create economic leverage.

In recent years there has been dissatisfaction with exchange rate mechanisms within the international monetary system. When exchange rates do not reflect underlying economic conditions, there may be misalignments among currencies. Fluctuations in rates have tended to be larger than would be expected, based upon different rates of inflation in the major industrialized countries. This introduces advantages or disadvantages that are not based on differences in underlying economic conditions (Hein, p. 14). The February 1987 Louvre Accord among the G-7 industrialized nations developed target zones for the major currencies. Upper and lower bounds were established against the dollar, within which the currencies could fluctuate. This has created a certain flexibility as the bounds can be modified over time, and there is no firm commitment to intervention should the bounds be exceeded. The system seems to have worked well, and regular meetings of the G-7 have studied the results and reaffirmed the agreement. Greater stability among exchange rates allows for better economic planning and decision making. With the development of the European Monetary System these relationships will be under critical evaluation;

the functioning of the international monetary sector will need to be closely monitored.

This is a time of enormous change in the world's financial markets, as a greater interdependency is being established. Widespread applications of advanced information and communication technologies to financial transactions have reduced the cost and increased the efficiency of acquiring and evaluating information. It is now possible to trade in a global market virtually around the clock, and the financial information and activity in Tokyo and London may be more important to New York traders than information from U.S. regional exchanges. There are a number of reasons for this. International bank lending and new international bond issues have grown more than twice as fast as GNP in the industrial countries in the 1980s. The ease with which currencies can be transferred in the international market allows investors to move their resources to the market with the highest interest rates. In recent years there has been greater use made of debt markets worldwide and also there have been a variety of new debt instruments available in the market. Deregulation of national financial markets has facilitated cross-border financial flows, the introduction of new security instruments, and larger foreign participation in domestic markets. As the world's capital markets become more integrated, they also become more interdependent. Repercussions, both positive and negative, can be quickly transferred to other exchanges. A sharp rise or fall in the New York market can be traced around the world, from Tokyo to London, and to several smaller exchanges, as well. This greater interdependency requires increased supervisory and regulatory action to protect the domestic as well as the foreign investor (see Hine, pp. 16–17). The establishment of a common capital market within the EC as part of the 1992 initiative will only add to this new worldwide financial market.

CONCLUSIONS

To discuss the major issues facing the international economic order in the 1990s and beyond is a challenging task. In a short essay it is possible to do little more than identify some of the changes which are occurring as international political and economic systems are in transition. Even some of these preliminary considerations will be affected by the Gulf crisis in ways that are only beginning to be addressed. Whatever the outcome, however, some conclusions can be drawn. The completion of the internal market in the European Community will create the largest trading bloc in the world. As other nations seek to relate to the EC, such as the EFTA nations, the countries of the Mediterranean and of Eastern Europe, the importance of this bloc will be enhanced. Traditional economic relationships between the East and West and between the North and South are being modified. This presents problems, but also opportunities which can be used to increase the benefits associated with regional development schemes. The need for investment funds has increased dramatically with the opening up of the economies of Eastern Europe. The industrialized world must bear greater responsibility for providing resources for growth and development, not only to the developing nations in the southern hemispheres, but also to the newly developing nations of Eastern Europe. Those nations impacted by the Gulf crisis will also need assistance.

Trade relationships form the core of the international economic system. As new economic units are formed, the negotiating positions in organizations such as GATT will be modified. Issues of concern to the triad powers will still be important, but the institutions will need to be more responsive to the needs of those nations and regions which have less economic power. Trading relationships are often a function of political structures, and so the two main trends, increased economic integration and improved trading relations, are closely linked in the developing economic order of the 1990s.

Globalization of the economic environment will also be increasingly significant. Dealing with problems and possibilities presented by stateless corporations, increasing population, and rapid changes in the financial sectors will require better understanding of how the systems operate. Creative thinking and increased planning will be necessary to meet the challenges of the new order and especially to avoid vulnerability at key sectors of the international economic environment.

There are problems to be faced in this changing economic and political environment, but there is also enormous potential in this developing economic order. The international economic system is becoming more integrated and thus more interdependent. The benefits of this could mean improved regional solutions to problems, though the Gulf war may call this hope into question. But a more interdependent world will also be a more complex—and more vulnerable—world requiring collective decision making through multilateral diplomacy. International politics and economics must be ever more closely interrelated in the 1990s and beyond.

BIBLIOGRAPHY

Books

Calingaert, Michael. *The 1992 Challenge from Europe: Development of the European Community's Internal Market*. Washington, D.C.: National Planning Association, 1988.

Hein, John. *Global Economic Trends: What Lies Ahead for the 90s*. New York: The Conference Board, Inc., 1989.

Owen, Richard and Dynes, Michael. *The Times Guide to 1992*. London: Times Books Limited, 1989.

Articles

Balakrishnan, N. "The Next NIC." *Far Eastern Economic Review*. 7 September 1989, pp. 96–100.

Broad, R. "No More NICs." *Foreign Policy* 72 (Fall 1988): 81–103.

Colvin, Geoffrey. "Gearing Up for the 90s: Trends to Watch." *NYU Business*, Fall 1989/Winter 1990, pp. 44–46.

Farnsworth, Clyde H. "Stalled Geneva Farm Talks Are Suspended for a Month." *New York Times*, 25 July 1990, p. D1.

Fleiss, Barbara A. "Geneva Round to Uruguay Round." *Europe* 296 (May 1990): 13–14.

Henderson, Hazel. "G-15: A Different Economic Summit." *The Christian Science Monitor*, 9 July 1990, p. 19.

Holstein, William J. "The Stateless Corporation." *Business Week*, 14 May 1990, pp. 98–105.

LaFranchi, Howard. "European Trade Groups Inch toward Accord." *The Christian Science Monitor*, 18 May 1990, p. 6.

Lewis, Flora. "The People Threat." *New York Times*, 14 July 1990, p. 21.

Riding, Alan. "Four European Nations Planning a New Focus on North Africa." *New York Times*, 30 July 1990, p. 5.

__________. "U.S. to Relax Standards on High-Tech Exports." *New York Times*, 8 June 1990, p. 46.

Rockwell, Keith M. "The Top Traders." *Europe* 296 (May 1990): 6–9.

Rowley, A. "Waning of the NICs?" *Far Eastern Economic Review*, 18 August 1988, p. 79.

Scherer, Ron. "Latin Plan Launches New Partnership." *The Christian Science Monitor*, 3 July 1990, p. 4.

Sommer, Mark. "G-7 Talks: Rebuilding Europe." *The Christian Science Monitor*, 9 July 1990, p. 18.

Interviews

On the subject of agriculture, interviews with EC Commissioner Ray MacSharry and Ambassador Julius Katz, deputy U.S. trade representative, as reported in *Europe* 297 (June 1990): 27–30.

CHAPTER SIX

The Information Revolution and the Shaping of a Democratic Global Order

DONALD L. CHATFIELD

INTRODUCTION

As political change sweeps across the globe, information systems increasingly play a key role in the reporting of events and in the actual accomplishment of reform. Breakthroughs in information technology now permit these systems to act as a major component in the reporting and shaping of world events. The use of facsimile transmission machines, worldwide computer networks, satellite transmission, and personal computers has transformed the manner in which global citizens receive news. More important, these breakthroughs also change the manner in which we *understand* world events.

I will argue in this chapter that the information revolution provides democratizing nations with the ability to break authoritarian propaganda machines and to avoid the development of the capitalist propaganda paradigm. The influence of such information-control mechanisms may be offset through a two-pronged approach. The first element requires the placement of fast and effective communication capability within the hands of all citizens. Communication capability of this nature involves the growth of telephone, radio, and computer conferencing networks in democratizing nations. The second element relates to the capacity for grass-roots organizers to employ information analysis techniques to address issues of public concern. Powerful analytic software packages now place significant analytical tools on the desktops of community organizers.

The Role of the Information Revolution in Global Democratization

Access to information and the ability to analyze its meaning has always played an important role in the shaping and maintenance of political power. In contrast to those who see information technology as yet another tool of oppression, I shall argue that the information revolution provides important opportunities for the shaping of a democratic global order. I will take issue with those communication scholars who believe that political states and corporations have developed manipulative mechanisms and will use the information revolution to ensure their continued power and influence. These scholars adhere to the propaganda model of information dissemination which, they maintain, provides insight into situations where a prevailing interest (government or industry), controls the release of information to serve its own ends. In the case of authoritarian regimes, the propaganda model considers state-run media outlets that are designed to further the aims of the ruling party. In capitalist societies, propaganda models are often applied to corporations which control media outlets. In either case, communication systems that are controlled by propaganda severely limit the ability of ordinary citizens to interpret events for themselves. In contrast to this model, I will argue that developments associated with the information revolution hold promise to replace this type of information control, placing new information in the hands of grass-roots organizations and citizens groups.

The primary beneficiaries of the information revolution will be world citizens. The new openness of information flow will make it increasingly difficult for governments to conceal the negative effects of their policies. The true impact of poverty, hunger, and environmental degradation will be made clear to citizens of societies impacted by the information revolution. Grass-roots organizations, also equipped with new information technologies, can make it clear that legitimate human needs must be addressed by government.

The information revolution also holds promise for officials and administrators of new democracies. As these leaders strive to establish a viable democratic structure, the information revolution offers several tools to analyze data related to new laws, environmental protection, and the provision of human services. These tools offer the potential for new democracies to work in concert with informed constituencies. Analytical software packages that formerly required a mainframe computer now operate on desktop systems. Many of these analytical tools have been utilized in Western democracies for decades, while others are currently under development. Due to the high cost of operation, these systems were previously reserved for use by government and industry. But breakthroughs in microcomputer technology now place powerful analytic tools in the hands of private citizens. The use of such information systems in countries undergoing democratization may assist the process of change and may help to ensure that the voices of all citizens are heard.

The Propaganda Model

Scholars who adhere to the propaganda model of information flow point to the ownership of media sources by multinational corporations. Ben Bagdikian calculated that 29 companies controlled the majority of world media outlets in 1987. He contends that the "antidemocratic potential of this emerging corporate control is a black hole in the mainstream media universe. . . . What the public learns is heavily weighted by what serves the economic and political interests of the corporations that own the media."[1]

Edward Herman and Noam Chomsky further elaborate on the notion of information flow as propaganda. They do not argue that such a model is based on conspiracy, but that the basic forces of a free-market economy encourage corporate media outlets to eliminate coverage that would harm business interests.

According to Herman and Chomsky, the basic elements of a propaganda model include:

1. the size, concentrated ownership, owner wealth, and profit orientation of the dominant mass-media firms;

2. advertising as the primary income source of the mass media;

3. the reliance of the media on information provided by government, business, and "experts" funded and approved by these primary sources and agents of power;

4. "flak" as a means of disciplining the media; and

5. "anticommunism" as a national religion and control mechanism.[2]

The release of information as propaganda is relatively easy to identify in authoritarian regimes where state media outlets closely monitor news stories. The war in the Persian Gulf offers examples of propaganda, as military censors on both sides of the conflict carefully control the flow of information from battle areas. Justified on this basis of national security, such propaganda is designed to meet the strategic aims of the government controlling the flow of information.

Herman and Chomsky admit that the existence of propaganda in a democratic society is much more difficult to identify since there is no formal censorship and no state-sanctioned media outlet. Propaganda, in capitalist countries, takes the form of news releases that mask the true activities of corporate entities. Those who adhere to this viewpoint, for example, point to biased news reports regarding the state of various world conflicts. By exaggerating the severity of political imbalance, the military-industrial complex is better able to justify large expenditures on weapons systems.

Those who are skeptical about the possibility for true democratic reform in the Soviet Union, Eastern Europe, and other quarters of the globe will undoubtedly argue that the capacity for this type of communication is dependent upon an economy that can sustain technological development and the purchase of sophisticated machinery. This chapter will also deal with questions related to communication trade policy, technology transfer agreements, and economic requirements to sustain the information revolution.

Most revolutions have to do with gunpowder, political intrigue, and military strategy. But the historic roots of this revolution involve primitive telegraph wires, telephone sets, crystal radios, and vacuum tubes. The foundations of the information revolution were developed in the late 1800s, but its evolutionary growth has taken place during this century. The information revolution is composed of three distinct components: the development of fast and reliable telecommunication systems, broadcast communication technology, and the development of computing devices for the analysis of data. Rapid advances in each of these areas within the past few decades have brought about new possibilities for application of information technology to the development of a global democratic order.

ISSUES OF THE INFORMATION REVOLUTION

Although the world has been linked by telephone, radio, and television for several decades, new technologies have created an increased capability for information flow. Improved communication, due to these new technologies, creates the potential for new democratic possibilities in international politics. The possibility for new openness through increased information flow can serve to counter the historical control of information by governments and corporate interests.

Technological Capabilities for Information Dissemination

Recent advances in the information revolution coincide with political upheaval in Eastern Europe, the transformation of the Soviet economy, conflict in the Persian Gulf, the struggle against apartheid in South Africa, and ecological struggle in South America. As we try to envision a future scenario that may result from these developments, the possibility exists for the information revolution to play a key role in the development of a new democratic global order.

Daniel Bell suggests that the political outline of the 21st century contains at least four points: the collapse of communism, the reunification of Europe, the end of the "American Century," and the rise of the Pacific rim.[3] The revolution in information technology affects each of these trends and, in many ways, augments them. The potential for the increased flow of information and the ability to quickly analyze large data sets creates the possibility for more intelligent decision making by a wider group of world citizens. Since large databases are routinely used by governmental planning agencies, the viewpoints of citizen groups have often been dismissed as ill informed. Now that these data sets can be analyzed on microcomputers, grass-roots organizations have increased power to challenge governmental decision making.

The information revolution also affords an opportunity to provide timely and accurate information to large groups of people without ideological filters. New information networks are developing that are highly decentralized and are resistant to the governmental and commercial pressures discussed by Herman and Chomsky. The speed of information delivery is critical for citizen action in highly charged political situations.

In order to break the dominance of the corporations which hold the majority of media outlets, as well as state-run media sources, citizens must have access to reliable and inexpensive communication technologies. Although business interests are clamoring to provide communication services to new democracies, there is much uncertainty about the future of global telecommunications. Since reliable telephone service is essential for computer networks, facsimile transmission, and teleconferences, the development of a global network will play a key role in the continued impact of the information revolution. The development of such a global network and the affordability of information technology is essential for this revolution to assist in efforts of democratization. When such a system is operational, the propaganda model of information flow can be replaced with a more flexible, decentralized network that gives greater voice to a pluralistic citizenry.

The war in the Persian Gulf raises new concerns about the effectiveness of global telecommunications systems during wartime. During the initial stages of the conflict, American-led forces were successful in disrupting major portions of the communications network in Iraq. This development, achieved in a matter of days by allied bombing, underscores the delicacy of the communications web which links the globe.

Affordability and Accessibility Issues

Can newly developing democracies sustain the technological growth necessary for information innovation without a free market? In nations attempting to develop a healthy economy, a key factor for democratization is the impact of economic pressures on access to information. Will new democracies be able to afford the technology necessary to become a part of the global communications network? Can nations afford the technology necessary to connect wider segments of their populations? Will citizens have the means to connect with these sources of information? Let us consider some of the more promising developments related to affordability and accessibility of information technology.

As early as 1978, the Organization for Economic Cooperation and Development (OECD) recognized the importance of equality in information access. Hans Gassman, senior official of the OECD, commented on the political importance of information accessibility:

> A system to which only financially powerful users have access must be avoided or international information networks, instead of contributing to the transparency of the world economic system, will make it more opaque and will increase existing disparities between the "information rich" and the "information poor."[4]

In the United States, a citizen may become part of the global computer network for a modest investment. Network users in the United States can utilize a toll-free telephone number to connect with an international network, a feature that is rare in developing countries. Until this type of accessibility can be developed, this cost of on-line computer communication will remain prohibitively high for most world citizens.

In countries where capitalism is taking tentative steps, there is uncertainty about the type of marketplace that will emerge. Bogdan Denitch fears that the rise of capitalism in Eastern Europe may lead to a less than desirable marketplace. Eastern European countries, he argues, must deal with a powerful state sector, a powerful and corrupt private sector, and pressure from the superpowers. He believes the result is likely to be a highly politicized market that will not respond adequately to the needs of citizens.[5] If his diagnosis is correct, some fear that the economies of newly free Eastern European nations may be slow to reach a point at which they sustain individual access to information technology. According to Denitch, the result may be that "the market economy will be subject to considerable corruption as former bureaucrats ... join foreign investors in a scramble to grab the more lucrative chunks of the economy."[6] The impact on information technology may be the limitation of affordable and accessible means of communication.

In spite of these concerns, there is significant evidence to indicate that new market economies will facilitate the information revolution by developing robust markets. For example, there is an impetus for improved East-West trade in communications goods. The formation of the European Community also signifies a strengthened ability for collective economic action. Research also indicates that residents of communist countries may be more willing to embrace capitalism than had been expected. Public opinion research conducted by Robert Schiller indicates that Soviet citizens are, in some cases, more open to capitalism than residents of New York. Schiller used a random telephone survey to poll 360 residents in New York and 360 Moscow residents. When asked if they would accept a tripling of upper class incomes in exchange for a 1 percent increase in all salaries, 49 percent of the Soviets agreed, while only 30 percent of the New Yorkers found that option acceptable. Soviet citizens were also more open to inflation, as long as their personal income continued to rise.[7] Some economists have speculated that residents of communist countries might be resistant to the development of free market economies because they would have to give up the certainties of guaranteed employment, housing, and medical care.[8] These survey results indicate that there may be much less resistance to the development of free markets, a development that is necessary to provide citizens with access to the global information network.

While citizens of communist countries may be open to capitalist markets, there is little doubt that the establishment of such markets will be gradual and sometimes painful. While the reach of information technology may be limited to certain sectors of the population during these formative years, the benefits of greater communication flow will be evident for all citizens. Collective groups of citizens, for example, may band together to afford access to telephone systems, computer conference networks, and other avenues in order to collect and disseminate information related to their purposes.

Global Trade Policies and Technology Transfer

Global trade policy and restrictions related to the international transfer of technology also pose potential obstacles for the information revolution. These policies have a direct impact on the accessibility of machinery and software that is capable of increasing information flow and data analysis. U.S. policy, in particular, is not adequately prepared to deal with issues related to technology transfer. American public policy has not yet addressed the commercial application of policy and no "agency of the federal government has broad responsibility for research and other activities related to civilian technology or for strategic coordination of technology policy at the national level."[9] As a result, high-level technology may be sheltered from international trade, even though it has no importance for military or strategic purposes.

Because of the strategic implications of information technology, the trade of communication and computing items has been especially susceptible to trade restrictions. In spite of the lack of coherent policy regarding such trade in the United States, historical events have provided an opportunity for the development of more open trade policies involving information technology. The period following World War II was marked by a movement to establish free trade between nations. The General Agreement on Tariffs and Trades (GATT) was signed in 1947, the agreement now includes 88 nations. GATT sought to establish trade without import tariffs and quotas.

Although the agreement is still intact, a number of practices have been established to circumvent its intent.[10]

A number of political developments in the United States have resulted in the limitation of trade related to information technology. Restrictive measures related to trade of information products include the U.S. Export Administration Act, the Buy American Act, and various export controls. The rationale for some of these trade limitations has to do with "militarily critical technology." The American position has been to limit the sale of technology to any country that might later use it against the United States in a war.

More attention has been given to the development of trade guidelines with potential rivals than has been given to the transfer of technology to developing nations. But the dissolution of the Eastern bloc may provide a window of opportunity to provide significant amounts of information technology to countries undergoing democratization. Provision of these capabilities would appear to be in the best interest of established democracies since information technology has the capacity to assist these countries in the more rapid development of democratic government. In this context, care could be taken to provide information technology that assists in establishing global community, rather than technology that develops further suspicion among nations.

As the elements of the information revolution become more affordable and accessible, opportunities to assist in the establishment of a global democratic order present themselves. Some of these opportunities already exist, while others are on the horizon.

OPPORTUNITIES FOR GLOBAL DEMOCRATIZATION

The combined power of the telecommunications revolution and the computing revolution provide many opportunities to help bring about a global democratic order. Innovations in information technology provide new opportunities to inform and empower citizen groups. By providing accessible information to individual citizens, new power is placed in the hands of an enlightened populace.

The information revolution also brings about opportunities for new democracies to borrow policy models from existing governments.

In the past, this type of policy exchange has been heavily dependent upon the influence of outside consultants, but new information systems enable decisionmakers to interpret and choose policy models based on their own analysis. This ability gives new democratic leaders the opportunity to develop more effective constitutions and laws that are appropriate for each political situation.

New opportunities for ecological protection and resource management are also important for formerly communist countries that now face enormous environmental problems. Once again, the resources of the information revolution provide important data about environmental issues and the ability to analyze individual problems. These environmental information systems have proven successful in established democracies and hold great promise for newly established democracies.

New Power in the Hands of an Informed Citizenry

The primary benefit of the information revolution for citizens of new democracies is the ability to provide information about the consequences of governmental action. As a result of the information revolution, the truth about poverty, environmental risks, labor policies, and community well-being is now available to a wider segment of the global population. This means that regimes are less able to hide the impacts of their policies. As with all revolutions, this creates new opportunities *and* risks for democracy.

Propaganda models of communication rely on hierarchical structures to distribute information. The information revolution allows networks to form in which information can flow through a variety of channels. Brian Murphy describes the networks as a decentralized system that "can be reordered dynamically. Choice decisions can be made anywhere within the network. It is no longer the prerogative of a controlling elite."[11]

A decentralized global information center is currently under development at the Walker Center for Ecumenical Exchange in Newton, Massachusetts. The Walker Center was founded in 1869 as a home for the children of missionaries and retired missionaries of the Lutheran Church. The global ties of its constituents have helped the center to develop three special programs to facilitate global information exchange. Gordon Schultz, director of the Walker Center, emphasizes the importance of placing information in the hands of the citizenry: "We work with grass-roots community groups to help them understand the complexity of the world and how the United States is changing."[12]

The Walker Center's China Information Center was developed in response to the May 1989 student protest in Tiananmen Square and provides current information about democratic efforts in the Republic of China. Following the Chinese government's crackdown in Tiananmen Square, the Walker Center used phone numbers of 30,000 fax machines in China to distribute news of the massacre. The center also smuggled a computer and modem into China in order to permit rapid communication without governmental interference. Gordon Schultz, director of the center, says: "This is something we can do: Serve as a springboard for people of these nations to spread their message to the world."[13]

The Walker Center also directs the Paths to Democracy program, formerly headed by Soviet dissident Andrei Sakharov. This program brings together leaders of democracy movements from many nations to discuss the ingredients necessary for a viable democratic system.[14]

The tools of the information revolution are indispensable to the work of the Walker Center. The center uses fax machines, computer databases, and computer bulletin boards to stay in contact with democratic organizers around the globe. Extensive use of electronic mail systems allows the rapid transmittal of documents and statements without governmental interference. Schultz once believed that technology was a tool of oppression, "but we couldn't function without it now. . . . For people with courage and imagination, technology can be an important tool."[15]

Other citizen groups around the world are forming similar alliances through the use of computer networks. One such network, PeaceNet, gives members a forum to communicate important political events in their area and to seek assistance in efforts for reform. Whether these grass-roots organizations utilize computer networks, facsimile transmission, or simple telephone communication, their networks undercut the foundation of the propaganda model of information dissemination.

Because these networks are decentralized, they are highly resistant to "flak" that might be introduced to confuse the issue. Computer networks are especially interactive, permitting the sort of independence that is needed to provide information to challenge prevailing authoritarian political orders.

Residents of formerly communist countries may find their newfound voices to be overwhelming. Residents of the United States are accustomed to a political system that affords extensive opportunities for public discussion and input. This system inherently makes policy-making a slow and arduous task, protecting our basic constitutional framework. But citizens who are anxious to see sweeping reforms in their governments may be unprepared for the tempests of public exchange. Increased efficiency in information flow may give citizens a public voice, but it may also result in a more conservative pace of reform.

The use of computerized analytical tools may further empower citizens who seek to establish democracy in their homeland. These situations provide the ideal opportunity for the practice of "participatory research." Participatory research is a strategy to involve citizens in the collection of data and the interpretation of its meaning in order to facilitate social change. Peter Park describes participatory research as "a framework in which people seeking to overcome oppressive situations can come to understand the social forces in operation and to gain strength in collective action."[16] The introduction of participatory research into citizen action groups recasts the traditional definition of research. Instead of a rigid and constraining process of quantification or analysis, participatory research sets the stage for creative discovery of knowledge and application to problems immediately at hand. This is not to say that participatory research is without standards. The model provides an educational process that enables the participants to handle basic elements of analysis, whether they be statistical measures or qualitative considerations. The flexibility of the approach does, however, provide a freedom to explore and experiment.

Participatory research attempts to place the power of research and understanding within reach of those most affected by social problems. The model's focus on the least free residents of our globe emphasizes the importance of placing information within their reach.

Rather than employing research techniques to study *about* the problems of the dispossessed, participatory research enables the dispossessed to discover the roots of their ills and thus motivates them to action.

Microcomputer-based database management systems, spreadsheet programs, statistical packages, and geographic information systems are examples of computer programs that might be used to help citizens find their voices in the public debate. These tools provide reliable analysis and place sophisticated techniques within the reach of grass-roots organizations. Software packages such as these can provide important educational benefits for the groups using them and will also add reliable data to the public discourse.

Ecological and Resource Management Opportunities

Environmental problems, particularly those that may create catastrophic global consequences, have engaged the attention of global decisionmakers. The potential loss of the world's rain forests, endangered plant and animal species, global warming trends, and air and water degradation have become timely issues in the United States and elsewhere in the world. With political upheaval in Eastern Europe, the world is now learning of ecological hazards within formerly communist countries.

Eastern European citizens may live under some of the world's worst environmental conditions. In their struggle for economic survival, these countries have invested less than 1 percent of their GNP in environmental protection (West Germany invested 3 percent of its 1988 GNP in environmental improvement). The result is an environmental disaster. It is estimated that Bitterfield, East Germany, has annual dust emissions of 40,000 tons and sulfur dioxide emissions of 90,000 tons.[17]

The tools of the information revolution may be used to address these problems. Information technology is available for citizen groups who need to stay informed about the true consequences of environmental degradation. Information systems are also available for the governments of new democracies to ensure that environmental problems are met with timely policy actions.

Environmental Computer Bulletin Boards.   As nations democratize, citizens will undoubtedly call for more investment in ecological protection.   But how will citizens stay informed of the hazards of environmental pollution?   One answer may lie in the computer bulletin board.   Systems like EcoNet, a worldwide environmental computer bulletin board, help to create opportunities for citizen involvement and political action.   With EcoNet, citizens concerned about ecological issues have formed a nonprofit computer conference network that connects environmentalists throughout the world.   The system requires a personal computer equipped with a modem and is accessible with a modest use fee.

Once the user makes a connection, he or she has access to several news services concerned with the environment and can participate in discussions and send messages around the globe.   The system has already provided members with a mechanism to distribute accurate information in a timely manner about various ecological crises.

When the Exxon tanker *Valdez* ran aground off coastal Alaska in 1989, the EcoNet system sprang into action with full accounts of the situation.   While the mass media was broadcasting optimistic reports about the severity of the spill and efforts to contain it, EcoNet provided current information about the reality of the situation.   One EcoNet member, a fisherman on the coast of Alaska, was the first to disseminate information about the lack of equipment to control the spill and the damage to beaches.   He reported that Exxon had hired every available boat for cleanup efforts, but that they were sitting idle in the harbor.[18]

In this manner, EcoNet was able to circumvent two of the basic elements of the propaganda model.   By relying on a citizen-based network of "reporters," the system reported news that was not colored by the interests of media corporations.   In addition, the network reported events based on motivations for environmental protection, not advertising revenue.   Systems like EcoNet offer disparate citizen groups the opportunity to share news that is timely and accurate, without the biases of the corporate media.   Computer conference networks, such as EcoNet, hold promising potential in developing countries as well.   Although the network is based in the

United States, participants on networks in 70 other countries have access to the service.

Geographic Information Systems. As environmental information spreads to citizens of new democracies, they are likely to demand an appropriate governmental response to ecological problems. Geographic information systems (GIS) provide analytical powers that can help new democracies address environmental problems. GIS technology can assist these countries by providing thorough analyses of environmental resources, natural and human constraints, and recommendations for action. These systems can also aid new democratic countries in the provision of human services by providing information related to economic development, the location of new housing, the need for medical facilities, and requirements for new schools. Although GIS technology has been limited to well-developed free-market economies, real opportunities exist for their use in new democracies.

A typical geographic information system has the capability to categorize several "layers" of computerized information. For example, a study to determine geographical areas at greatest environmental risk might utilize the following layers of data:

- a map of the study area, including roadways, mountain ranges, and other special features;

- geological information;

- air and water quality data;

- an inventory of plant life; and

- rainfall amounts by region.

With this information, the GIS could then generate information about the interrelationship of these factors. The system could then determine those geographic areas that are most in need of policy interventions.

Microcomputers will support many GIS programs, making this technology affordable and accessible for new governments. These systems are especially valuable because they can forecast the result of environmental policy decisions, based on system data. This means that several policy alternatives can be explored to determine the action that will best accomplish environmental protection.

Remote Sensing Systems. Remote sensing technology is yet another innovation that might assist new democracies as they attempt to correct environmental problems. One example of a remote sensing system is the Global Positioning System (GPS). GPS is a satellite-based network that provides accurate, three-dimensional geographic positions anywhere on the earth's surface. Applications of the system have demonstrated its maps to be accurate within two centimeters, a remarkable achievement since the information is collected from a space-based camera. The technology was originally developed by the U.S. Department of Defense for military navigational systems. The effectiveness of the system has been demonstrated in the Persian Gulf war. Using information from space-based satellites, allied bombers have been able to target specific facilities in a highly accurate manner. When Saddam Hussein began dumping oil into the Persian Gulf, for example, satellite data was used to guide a bomb through the vent of a pumping station to stop the flow of oil.

In addition to important strategic uses, GPS technology is also important in many nonmilitary endeavors. The system is now accessible to civilian groups, opening the potential for a number of applications. Eight GPS satellites are currently in operation, with plans for a 20-satellite network by 1992. These satellites are continually tracked from five GPS ground stations operated by the Department of Defense. Civilian users may utilize the network through a GPS receiver. While this technology may sound far-fetched, the proponents of GPS envision it as the next "utility," much as telephones are a utility. Users of the system claim that "[w]ith today's integrated circuit technology GPS receivers are fast becoming small enough and cheap enough to be carried by just about anyone."[19]

The applications of citizen-based research for GPS data have thus far been limited to the United States. Shared data agreements could provide important information to countries with severe environmental problems. Areas of Eastern Europe that are plagued by environmental problems could utilize GPS data to establish priorities for environmental cleanup efforts, in a form of ecological triage.

Exchange of Policy Models

The information revolution helps to give citizens new power by providing them with accurate information, and also provides means for grass-roots organizations to mobilize to deal with environmental problems. But the benefits of the information revolution may also be used by the governments of new democracies to ensure long-term viability.

As Eastern European countries seek to democratize their governing apparatus, they often look to the West for existing models. Anne Schneider and Helen Ingram label this practice the systematic "pinching" of policy ideas. In order to design policy in accordance with the needs of specific social and economic circumstances, political leaders often borrow policies that have worked well in similar conditions.[20] In many cases, these countries rely on the interpretation and recommendation of Western policy experts.

For example, Czechoslovakia employed U.S. attorneys to assist in the development of its new constitution. Eric Stein, emeritus professor of law at the University of Michigan, was part of an international committee formed to assist Czechoslovakia in the writing of a new constitution. Another team from the Johns Hopkins University Institute for Policy Studies provided guidance for new local government officials on the administration of their posts.[21] In these cases, Czechoslovakian officials were dependent upon the interpretation of American consultants as they "borrowed" policy appropriate to the unique needs of Czechoslovakia. While this type of relationship has proven helpful for developing democracies, the information revolution provides opportunities to borrow policy models in a more autonomous fashion. Many opportunities exist for developing democracies to "borrow" policy ideas through avenues provided by information technology.

The practice of borrowing policies that have proven successful for other governments is common among local jurisdictions in the United States. New openness in the flow of information has increased the speed at which jurisdictions learn of new policy designs and innovations. These communication opportunities provide wide opportunities for developing nations to do the same. The use of telecommunications capabilities, computer conferences, and facsimile machines provide new democracies opportunities to compare policy designs, not just with established democracies, but with other nations in similar situations. Traditional forms of information delivery, such as mail and messenger service, will become increasingly less useful as more agencies are connected to computer communication networks.

An evolving technology in the United States, issues management systems (IMS) may hold promise for policy analysis in countries facing rapid democratization. This tool has the capacity to assist new democratic administrations to provide for the long-term success of policy structures. Issues management systems are capable of isolating "policy clusters" within existing legislation and can demonstrate policy inconsistencies and overlaps.

Issue management technology makes use of a database for existing legislation. During the process of German reunification, for example, East German officials may turn their attention to environmental laws. These policymakers could obtain copies of environmental legislation from the Federal Republic of Germany and representative states in the United States. When the statutes are integrated into the issues management software, policy designers may select "policy clusters" for consideration.

The system uses a key-word search to identify groupings of policy related to certain issues. In this case, a search might be undertaken for policy related to "coal-fired emissions standards." The system locates all legislation related to this issue and provides a report to the user. The user then determines which policy mechanisms would be useful according to the specific political setting. In this manner, local decisionmakers may quickly compare the other regulatory mechanisms in order to design guidelines that make sense for their own political situation. In this scenario, officials of new democracies literally have the collected policy of established democracies at their fingertips. They are empowered to borrow policy models that make the most sense for their constituents.

Although this type of analysis may not be completely new to Eastern European nations or the Soviet Union, the microcomputer revolution adds a new dimension. The increased power of desktop computing systems, previously reserved for central planning bureaucracies, can also place analytical power in the hands of community organizers. The availability of this tool to grass-roots organizers will increase the public debate about policy options and will allow even more policy alternatives to be considered.

DANGERS TO GLOBAL DEMOCRATIZATION

What might be the stumbling blocks that could slow the impact of the information revolution on democratization efforts? Information technology places new power within reach of the world's least free citizens, a development that may be resisted by some governments. This technology allows citizens to intelligently question the process of democratization. Such power may be suspect by older regimes undergoing reform and by totally new governing bodies.

Questions about information control and national security, real and imagined, will certainly be raised. In some cases, these concerns will be thinly disguised attempts to control information for the ends of the ruling party. In a similar fashion, issues about information control may be used to impede the progress of democratization. Communication theory refers to these issues as "gatekeeping" concerns. As new channels of information flow are established, will new methods of governmental and corporate control also be established? The development of new gatekeepers may minimize the impact of information technology. Finally, concern about the integrity of information may hinder the impact of the information revolution in the process of democratization. Conflicts characterized by many discordant voices raise legitimate questions about the quality of information received, especially data from a decentralized information network. How will the information revolution provide checks to ensure the quality of information received?

Security Issues

Nation-states routinely weigh the balance between the need for national control and individual rights. This question has historically been an issue of internal control, but the information revolution injects an added element. The increased flow of information gives external interests the ability to exercise certain measures of control and influence. Multinational corporations, for example, have the power to shape political opinion through their business communications across international borders.

As a result, one of the primary security issues involved with the information revolution deals with a phenomenon known as "transborder data flow." The United Nations defines these occurrences as "movements across national boundaries of machine-readable data for processing, storage or retrieval."[22] As this information flow began to develop, some countries voiced concern that such data flow undermined national security. Some leaders of developing countries believe that this flow of data may place them at a competitive disadvantage with outside governments and corporations. Other national leaders believe that the free flow of information across national borders may destabilize their societies and lead to revolution.[23]

Security concerns are based on two functional attributes of new information technology. The user of these information systems can control functions at a distance, including the actions of employees, machinery, or a corporation. Information technology also involves an immediate response, with no opportunity for outside intervention or scrutiny.[24] As discussed earlier, these capabilities provide opportunities for citizens and governments seeking more democratic models. Many established governments, however, find the speed and autonomy of these systems threatening.

These concerns are heightened because the strongest world economic markets are those with greatest access to information technology. The information revolution has developed more fully in the United States, Western Europe, and the Pacific Rim.[25] This means that multinational firms based in these areas may have an impact on the markets and the ideas of other nations.

The speed of information technology also concerns some governmental leaders. Traditional methods of communication, whether they be newspapers, television broadcasts, or books, take time to produce and are subject to some type of control before release to the general public. Today's information technology provides immediate release of current news and data, with no opportunity for governmental intervention or interpretation.

Four countries (Sweden, Brazil, Canada, and France) have taken steps to protect themselves from the perceived dangers of transborder data flows. These actions include controls on broadcast communications, data processing activities, and external databases. The measures are designed primarily to shield these nations from foreign dominance in economic and technological arenas. Other countries, including Mexico, Algeria, and Venezuela, have also taken steps to establish national policy about information issues.

Although concerns about national security are certainly understandable, further regulation of transborder data flow might significantly limit the potential benefits of the information revolution. When the transfer of data is tied to certain political or corporate interests, the resulting communication network is once again subject to the pressures of the propaganda model described by Herman and Chomsky. In order to protect national economic interests, while preserving the benefits of freely flowing information, new international agreements must be developed to ensure these goals. While the groundwork has already been laid for such agreements by several international organizations, creative formulations will be required to frame appropriate safeguards.

Gatekeeping Issues

In countries where rapid democratization is unfolding, questions remain about the interest of leaders in controlling information flow and dissemination. As state-run information agencies become more open, new forms of informational gatekeeping are certain to emerge. Communication theory recognizes that certain organizations, including political entities, employ methods to control the introduction of new information. In order to enter the system's communication system, "information must appear in a guise that is acceptable to the system's 'gatekeepers,' who make the initial determination of data appropriate to the system's needs."[26] Depending upon the level of control within the system, information then passes through a number of other gates where it is "edited" to further reflect the nature of the system. The highly interactive nature of new information technology makes traditional gatekeeping more difficult, but organizational behavior suggests that new forms will emerge.

Will reformers feel the need to retain control of information in order to achieve their social agenda? In the wake of new opportunities for information exchange, citizens should be aware of potential responses that might negate expected benefits. One such significant opportunity arose in July 1990 when Soviet President Mikhail Gorbachev issued a presidential order that Soviet radio and television outlets would be operated "independently of political and social organizations" to provide "impartial and thorough" coverage of national events.[27] Throughout Gorbachev's campaign for reform, the Soviet media has given him wide coverage and favorable reviews.

The presidential order appears to provide a new opportunity for increased communication of pluralistic views. Gorbachev's restructuring of broadcast outlets, however, did not make it "immediately clear whether or to what degree he might intend to cede this advantage of incumbency."[28] In other words, President Gorbachev seems to retain the power of the press to advance his own political agenda. A companion order also gave his Kremlin Cabinet the power to cancel unilateral decisions by local governments to change television outlets.[29] This order indicates that the art of governmental gatekeeping is alive and well in the Soviet Union.

One response to the problem of gatekeeping is the growth of personal computer networks. In 1986 it was estimated that there were 30,000 computer systems in the Soviet Union, ranging from microcomputers to mainframes. The 1985 Soviet Five-Year Plan called for an 80 percent increase in the production of computer systems.[30] If these targets are met, and if Western trade agreements with the Soviet Union continue to open communication and computer trade opportunities, citizens will have increased access to the basic components of the information revolution. If Soviet citizens continue to gain greater access to personal computers, printers, modems, facsimile machines, and the like, they will be able to assemble an information network that is more resistant to traditional gatekeeping tactics.

Issues of Informational Integrity and Privacy

As vast amounts of information become available to global citizens, new concerns arise about the dangers of data manipulation and corruption. Serious consideration should be given to new safeguards to allow the empowerment of information consumers.

Issues of informational integrity also relate to the privacy of individual citizens. Governments and multinational corporations routinely maintain large databases with comprehensive files on individuals. As the information revolution increases the capacity to cross national borders with personal data files, some citizens have voiced concern about the protection of their privacy and the integrity of information collected about them.

Many U.S. citizens think of privacy as a basic constitutional right. For American citizens, privacy of information is protected by 15 pieces of federal legislation, including the Privacy Act of 1974. The Privacy Act pertains to civilian federal record systems and provides limits on the information collected, rights to access and review information, and the establishment of management responsibility.[31] This type of legislation not only protects the privacy of citizens, but attempts to ensure the integrity of collected data.

The Council of Europe and the Organization for Economic Cooperation and Development have been active in the development of laws that are designed to provide restrictions on the use of private information about individual citizens and organizations. The OECD released guidelines that seek to provide free information flow while protecting the privacy of citizens:

> We are determined to advance the free flow of information between member countries and to avoid the creation of unjustified obstacles to the development of economic and social relations among member countries. However, because of the need for privacy protection, there should be space for exceptions to the free flow principle.[32]

Unless similar provisions are made in newly emerging democracies, individual citizens may feel justified in their concern about personal data collected by information networks. The integrity of information flow must be maintained in order to provide appropriate levels of privacy for individual citizens.

CONCLUSIONS AND IMPLICATIONS

The global information revolution influences both the flow of information and the manner in which it is analyzed. Governments have historically possessed the ability to control information for propaganda purposes. More recently, corporations have also developed this capacity. The information revolution, however, shows promise to offset the control mechanisms of both governments and corporations. New patterns of information dissemination follow highly decentralized networks, rather than the old hierarchical structure. As a result, communication becomes more interactive, with less opportunity for governmental or corporate intrusion. The absence of "noise" in new communication networks permits the flow of information with fewer ideological filters and allows citizen groups to grasp a more accurate picture of political events.

Computer programs for information analysis previously have been utilized primarily by government agencies and corporations. Now, however, the microcomputer revolution makes it possible for grass-roots organizations to utilize powerful analytical programs for organizational and educational purposes. These programs include issues management systems, statistical analysis packages, and geographical information systems. When combined with computer conference networks, these tools may serve as effective means for citizen organization across wide geographical areas. The use of these computer programs may enhance efforts in the area of participatory research whereby citizens are made more aware of the structures which cause oppression. These analytical packages also provide information that is free from corporate or governmental influences.

In order to provide developing democracies with access to information technology and data networks, trade agreements and technology transfer policies must be revised. The basic framework for an open trading environment is provided by the General Agreement on Tariffs and Trade of 1947, but efforts should be made to clarify subsequent policy that circumvents the agreement. The issue of technology transfer to developing Third World nations should also be studied more carefully in order to establish a consistent policy that will provide the tools for building democracy.

The information revolution provides many opportunities that may aid countries in the process of democratization. Improved information flow provides citizens with greater access to information about the activities of their governments. This information can illuminate the consequences of policy, making the specter of governmental abuse more difficult to conceal. Citizen groups are also empowered to propose reforms and structural changes through the use of decentralized communication networks. The addition of many voices to the policy debate may initially create confusion in these situations, but the overall effect will provide a system in which competing viewpoints are heard. Analytical tools, such as the issues management system, provide new governments with greater options as they seek to build and strengthen democratic systems.

"Revolutionary" activities often create social uncertainties, and the information revolution has created its share of concerns. Among the primary issues are those related to national security, personal privacy, and the development of new information gatekeepers. Security concerns may be handled through the effective use of international trade agreements, but the development of these compacts will be time-consuming. The United States, among other countries, must come to terms with the commercial and technical implications of communication technology spawned by military research. New trade policies must differentiate clearly between trade related to tools of destruction as opposed to technology that can engender a more interdependent global community.

The war in the Persian Gulf raises concerns regarding our reliance upon modern telecommunications capabilities. Intensive bombing of Iraq during the early stages of the war demonstrated the fragility of these networks. Disruption of telephone communication alone complicates communication via voice networks, facsimile machines, and computer modems. The relatively quick impact on Iraq's communications systems indicates susceptibility to communications sabotage for virtually every nation. The vulnerability of our communications systems underscores the need to establish reliable networks, resistant to external threats.

Personal privacy is valued differently in various cultures, but existing treaties have established a firm foundation for transborder data flow. Every effort should be made to include new democracies in the umbrella organizations that oversee the integrity of data transfer. The Organization for Economic Cooperation and Development provides an excellent framework for the integration of newly developed information societies.

As the information revolution continues to shatter the hierarchical structure of information flow, dangers may develop in the form of new data gatekeepers. While gatekeepers in the propaganda model tend to be government agencies, corporations, and media outlets, new gatekeepers may take the form of special interest groups or grass-roots organizations. The potential for these groups to develop propaganda techniques is limited by the structure of new communications networks. A larger gatekeeping issue has to do with national communication policy and international competitiveness. As free-market economies struggle to establish business in new markets, nations must be on guard against the possibility of exclusionary agreements that limit access to certain information networks. The formation of such exclusionary networks could serve to limit the accessibility of information to individual citizens.

The information revolution continues to play a role in the exhilarating pace of political change in the early 1990s and promises to shape future political events. Information technology provides tremendous power to enhance the efforts of government, business, and citizens groups. This potential may be harnessed to positive or negative efforts related to global democratization efforts. The opportunities are significant and hold promise to provide a more equitable global communication system in which information may be used to give voice to the oppressed and to make the impact of governmental policy readily apparent to its constituents.

ENDNOTES

1. Ben H. Bagdikian, *The Media Monopoly*, 2nd ed. (Boston: Beacon Press, 1987, p. x.

2. Edward S. Herman and Noam Chomsky, *Manufacturing Consent: The Political Economy of the Mass Media* (New York: Pantheon Books), 1988, p. 2.

3. Daniel Bell, "As We Go Into the Nineties: Some Outlines of the Twenty-First Century," *Dissent*, Spring 1990, p. 171.

4. Cited in Brian M. Murphy, *The International Politics of New Information Technology* (London: Croom Helm, 1986), p. 185.

5. Bogdan Denitch, "The Triumph of Capitalism?" *Dissent*, Spring 1990, p. 118.

6. Ibid., p. 178.

7. Peter Passell, "Does Gorbachev Know Best?" *The New York Times*, 18 July 1990, p. C2. The research was undertaken by Robert J. Schiller, an economist at Yale University; Maksim Boiko, a Soviet economist; and Vladimir Korobov, a Soviet sociologist. The results were presented to the National Bureau of Economic Research conference in Cambridge, Massachusetts, on 18 July 1990.

8. Ellen K. Coughlin, "Similarities Noted in U.S., Soviet Views of Free-market Economy," *The Chronicle of Higher Education*, 15 August 1990, pp. A5-A6.

9. B. R. Inman and Daniel F. Burton, Jr., "Technology and Competitiveness: The New Policy Frontier," *Foreign Affairs* 69, no. 2, p. 129.

10. Brian M. Murphy, *The International Politics of the New Information Technology* (London: Croom & Helm, 1986), p. 156.

11. Ibid., p. 264.

12. Patricia Harris and David Lyon. "Digitizing Democracy," *CompuServe Magazine*, July 1990, p. 39.

13. Ibid., p. 38.

14. Ibid.

15. Ibid., p. 39.

16. Peter Park, *What is Participatory Research? A Theoretical and Methodological Perspective* (Amherst, Massachusetts: Unpublished monograph, May 1989), p. 3. For an example of participatory research in action, see Orlando Fals-Borda, *Knowledge and People's Power: Lessons with Peasants in Nicaragua, Mexico and Columbia* (New York: New Horizons Press, 1988).

17. George D. Leal, "What About Eastern Europe?" *Elements* 19, no. 2, p. 1.

18. David Phinney, "Environmental Bulletin Board: EcoNet," *Computerland Magazine*, March/April 1990, p. 22.

19. Jeff Hurn, *GPS: The Next Utility* (Sunnyvale, California: Trimble Navigation, 1989), p. 9.

20. Anne Schneider and Helen Ingram, "Systematically Pinching Ideas: A Comparative Approach to Policy Design," *Journal of Public Policy* 8:61-80. See also, Helen Ingram and Anne Schneider, "Improving Implementation through Policy Design: Framing Smarter Statutes" (a paper presented to the American Political Science Association annual convention, Washington, D.C., September 1988).

21. Julie L. Nicklin, "Countries in East Europe Turn to American Professors for Help in Reshaping Governments and Economies," *The Chronicle of Higher Education* 36, no. 43, p. A10.

22. United Nations Center on Transnational Corporations, *Transborder Data Flows: Access to International On-Line Data Base Market: A Technical Paper* (New York, 1983), as cited by David Blatherwick in *The International Politics of Telecommunications* (Berkeley: University of California Institute of International Studies, 1987).

23. David E. S. Blatherwick. *The International Politics of Telecommunications* (Berkeley: University of California Institute of International Studies, 1987, p. 3).

24. Ibid.

25. Ibid.

26. Jerry W. Koehler, et al. *Organizational Communication: Behavioral Perspectives* (New York: Holt, Rinehart and Winston, 1976), p. 45.

27. Francis X. Clines of *The New York Times*, "Gorbachev Pulls Plug on TV, Radio Monopoly," in *The Arizona Daily Star*, 16 July 1990, p. 1.

28. Ibid.

29. Ibid.

30. Brian M. Murphy, p. 281.

31. Laudon and Laudon, pp. 575-76.

32. The Organization for Economic Cooperation and Development, *Guidelines Governing the Protection of Privacy and Transborder Data Flows of Personal Data* (adopted 23 September 1980 by a

vote of 18-0 with 6 abstentions), as cited in Brian Murphy, p. 195.

Conclusion

NEAL RIEMER

I. INTRODUCTION

What, finally, can we conclude about "New Thinking and Developments in International Politics: Opportunities and Dangers"? Most certainly, the world is experiencing momentous change. But what will be the character of the new world of international politics? As we respond to these questions, we must be careful not to be foolishly obsessed by the war in the Persian Gulf that broke out on 16 January 1991, and by our legitimate concerns about the postwar settlement in the Middle East. These matters are certainly most important for understanding important problems of the post–Cold War world, and key aspects of the new world of international politics. But these matters can be best understood in the larger light of the momentous events of 1990 around the globe.

II. GORBACHEV, EUROPE, AND THE WEST

Clearly, Gorbachev's political philosophy of perestroika and glasnost—whether a deeply articulated philosophy of socialism that is democratic, humane, and effective or a pragmatic response to economic and political malaise in the Soviet Union—has been instrumental in bringing the Cold War to a close. His political philosophy, even if we question some of his recent domestic actions as repressive, has enhanced the prospects of peaceful East-West relations and facilitated the end of authoritarian communist regimes in Eastern Europe. It has opened the door to the reunification of Germany and even made possible an invigorated United Nations. These several developments are politically significant breakthroughs in international politics. They present promising opportunities for creative leaders in Europe and the United States to act to consolidate these breakthroughs. Such consolidation is essential to ensure the long-term security of all European nations and the advent, in time, of constitutional democracies and prosperous economies throughout all of Europe.

Scholars will long debate the reasons for Gorbachev's new thinking and these momentous changes, as they will also debate the present reality and future prospects of domestic liberalization in the Soviet Union. They will also hotly debate the West's role in bringing about the end of the Cold War and the favorable consequences that flow from the end of the Cold War. However, even if the fuller program of perestroika and glasnost falters and fails, three key points are incontrovertible. Crucial breakthroughs have occurred. They present historic opportunities for security, freedom, and prosperity. Real dangers are not absent in East-West relations, in Europe, at the United Nations, in the Middle East, and around the globe.

The dangers in Europe must not be overlooked. Gorbachev's efforts to advance perestroika and glasnost could fail. Even if Gorbachev—or a comparable leader—stays in power in the Soviet Union, the paths to economic reform (including the introduction of features of a market economy) and to a Soviet variety of democratic socialism are strewn with serious obstacles. Comparable obstacles obstruct the efforts of the newly freed nations of Eastern Europe to establish working constitutional democracies and efficient and prosperous economies. Even the unification of Germany will encounter difficult times as two different political and economic systems merge. Western Europe, too, as it seeks a new security arrangement to replace a NATO that has lost its original *raison d'etre*, or as it seeks to advance fuller economic and political integration in 1992, will still need to struggle hard to work out new international patterns to make Europe whole and free.

Despite difficulties and dangers ahead, especially for the Soviet Union and most nations of Eastern Europe, the prospects for improved East-West relations and for European security, freedom, and prosperity are nonetheless highly promising. It appears that the Cold War, which dominated East-West relations after World War II, is being replaced, and rapidly, by an emerging new order of the post–Cold War world. We do not yet have a name for this new world of international politics, but it will certainly be a new world in important respects. Is it premature to call it an emerging constitutional global order?

Whatever we call this new world, it is clear that it is imperative to articulate—lucidly—the new policies that will guide this new world, and to be thinking—prophetically—of the consequences flowing from these new policies. Most tantalizing here is the possibility of the extension of the policy of economic integration in Western Europe to embrace all of Europe, including at some later date even the Soviet Union. Such economic integration—in conjunction with coordinated political, social, and ecological measures—might demonstrate the possibility of the end of catastrophic great power rivalries in Europe. Such measures might—just might—succeed in transcending, finessing, or constitutionalizing troublesome national ambitions and disputes that have been the bane of Europe in the 20th century. Such measures—as they enhance both national security and economic prosperity—might lend enormous support to both the prophetic argument on behalf of *shalom* and the pragmatic argument that peace is more rewarding, and less costly, than war. However, whether patterns of integration can be worked out in the absence of such an integrating glue as anticommunism remains to be seen.

The demise of anticommunism as a rallying cry in the Western world and the Soviet Union's seeming rejection of support for revolutionary violence in the Third World have important consequences in international politics. On one hand, such demise and such rejection could lead to a decline of militarism, arms shipments, unholy political alliances, and change by violent means. On the other hand, ironically, they could lead to neglect of problems, particularly problems of violence, in the Third World. At this time, it is too early to ascertain with confidence which scenario will play out. However, it is not premature to press vigorously for an end to outrageous arms shipments to militaristic, authoritarian regimes.

III. A NEW AND INVIGORATED UNITED NATIONS

New thinking and developments in East-West relations also hold out enormous promise for an invigorated United Nations. Assuming Chinese agreement, such a United Nations would be able (because of the unanimity of the great powers in the Security Council and elsewhere) to help bring peace to troubled areas of the world and to attend to such other crucial global problems as economic and social development in the developing world. Cooperative Soviet-American international action is, obviously, crucial to U.N. success. Even if the "peace and justice" dividend may not yet—for a number of reasons, especially the war in the Persian Gulf—be available for purposes of domestic reform, it is certainly the case that an invigorated United Nations is in fact already one tangible "peace and justice" dividend! The U.N. Security Council's prompt and resolute response to the Iraqi invasion of Kuwait is a dramatic illustration of a strong U.N. response to naked aggression. The Security Council not only condemned the invasion, but also called for strong economic sanctions against Iraq, and endorsed the use of force to secure compliance with U.N. resolutions. Such action by the Security Council, if historically rare, is tremendously encouraging. It holds out hope for a United Nations able to fulfill its original mission. However, the strong leadership role of the United States in opposing Iraq's invasion of Kuwait, and in leading the coalition war effort to drive Iraq out of Kuwait, must not be overlooked. Difficult and troubling questions need to be addressed here. Will the United Nations be effective in advancing the goal of collective security in the absence of strong American leadership? Will the United Nations be happy about the precedent established by an American-led war in accord with U.N. resolutions? What will be the shape of the postwar security arrangement in the Persian Gulf and the Middle East?

In this regard, however, it is also important to bear in mind that the more regular role for the United Nations will still be its third-party activity. Such activity will focus on important conflicts less prominent than the Iraqi invasion of Kuwait and theft of Kuwaiti assets. In addition, we can look forward to the increasing salience of the U.N.'s international "regimes" in dealing with a host of key problems relating to the environment, drugs, disease, and other issues.

Moreover, if the Soviet Union, Eastern Europe, Western Europe, and the United States have a vital interest in a European success story, and may—therefore—be relatively less disposed to address problems of developing nations of the southern hemisphere, an invigorated United Nations will most certainly press for greater efforts to address Third World problems. Greater attention to these Third World problems is another modest "peace and justice" dividend, even if funds to deal with them (given especially the huge expenditures caused by the war in the Persian Gulf) will not easily be forthcoming.

The problem of attaining funds to achieve a "peace and justice" dividend that could be applied to pressing domestic problems in such countries as the Soviet Union or the United States, or to the developing nations of the Third World, or to reconstruction in war-devastated lands, is intimately related to a peaceful and economically stable world. But will peoples and nations throughout the world see how the Iraqi invasion of Kuwait, and the subsequent war in the Persian Gulf, can upset not only regional but global peace, and require the allocation to military purposes and policing of monies that could be used for domestic reform in the United States, or to support U.S. or U.N. action on behalf of Third World peoples? Will the people of Iraq, or the peoples of other Arab countries who support Saddam Hussein, realize the costs of militaristic aggression in terms of military casualties, horrendous wartime destruction, and the exhaustion of funds that could be expended for beneficial social purposes? Will the peoples and leaders of other heavily armed, militaristic regimes come to similar conclusions? Here we are less confident of affirmative answers.

IV. THE PERSISTENCE OF VIOLENT CONFLICT IN INTERNATIONAL POLITICS

The peaceful settlement of all conflicts is, unfortunately, not yet at hand. Violent conflicts persist in the international system of the 1990s. Iraq's invasion of Kuwait in August 1990 and the outbreak of the American-led war against Iraq on 16 January 1991, are only the most dramatic reminder of such violence, which threatens to erupt, or has erupted, in a host of persistent disputes around the globe. Local wars—whether in Cambodia (Kampuchea) or Ethiopia or Somalia—still rage throughout the world. Because the stakes in these conflicts are not as ominous for the fate of mankind as the catastrophe of nuclear war fought by the superpowers, leaders and peoples in many developing countries have not yet seen the need to reject these conflicts. Creative leadership is taxed to articulate cost/benefit analyses designed to highlight the human and economic tragedy of such conflicts, to stop the flow of arms that feeds so many of these conflicts, and to adopt policies designed to reduce such conflicts to a minimum.

But how is it possible to constitutionalize these disputes—that is, to ensure that they will be resolved in peaceful and orderly ways? That question—and the search for creative breakthroughs to overcome such violence—must surely be on the policy agenda of creative leaders of the new world of international politics. In the emerging world of international politics it would be naive to believe that differences, disagreements, clashes of interest will disappear. But it is realistic—not naive—to press for constitutional mechanisms to resolve such disputes before they become lethal. Moreover, it is realistic to reassess a questionable U.S. balance of power policy (as in the Iraq-Iran war) and to look now, in the light of the war to drive Iraq out of Kuwait, to a policy of collective security, preferably under an invigorated United Nations. Such a policy would seek to safeguard Middle East states against aggression, protect vital economic interests and the international economy, and address—constitutionally—political and economic grievances.

A comparable question about the constitutionalization of disputes must be asked about terrorism. What democratic and constitutional steps can be taken to deal with the underlying causes of terrorism? Pending peaceful solutions, what can the global community do to prevent or counter terrorist violence in the world? The end of the Cold War, the decline of Soviet support for violent revolution around the globe, a cut-off of support for terrorists by oil-rich Arab states—these measures would help enormously. But it is by no means apparent that Libya or Iraq or Syria are ready to join a democratic and constitutional world order. And it is by no means obvious that terrorist organizations—or all those committed to armed struggle to achieve their objectives (whether in the Middle East or in Northern Ireland or elsewhere) are prepared to abandon violence in favor of peaceful and constitutional methods. We can, however, be heartened by the recent decision by Nelson Mandela and the African National Congress to abandon armed struggle in the campaign to overcome apartheid. And we can press vigorously to curtail arms sales, to limit military buildups, and to outlaw the manufacture and sale of biological and chemical weapons.

As nations move toward greater civility in international politics, they may in time be able to concentrate their attention on a different kind of battle—the battle against drugs and against international drug merchants. Already there is modest evidence at the United Nations and elsewhere of concentration on this different kind of battle.

V. THE IMPACT OF INTERNATIONAL ECONOMICS ON INTERNATIONAL POLITICS

The movement toward European integration—a significant breakthrough in its own right—has already served to help overcome traditional nation-state rivalries in Western Europe. The extension of such patterns of economic integration in Europe, in the Mediterranean, in the Americas, and elsewhere in the world needs to be encouraged. This movement holds out hope—as do related movements for freer global trade and for the globalization of business—that mutually beneficial economic arrangements can reduce nationalistic rivalries that have led to war and economic depression. The movements toward economic interdependence are, in the judgment of many keen economists, irreversible. They promise to tie nations together in economic bonds that will enhance prosperity. Policymakers, however, have to seek to ensure that such movements function to narrow—and not widen—the gap between rich and poor nations.

The plight of poorer peoples in developing nations is real. It would seem, however, that this plight can be most sensibly addressed in a peaceful, constitutional, and pragmatic world—in which swords are indeed beaten into plowshares and spears into pruning hooks; in which constitutional and democratic systems ensure security, freedom, and justice; and in which—given peace—monies can be used to address the key issues of development, with the highest priority going to human needs. But can this prophetic vision be realistically addressed in a world that often calls for striking balances between competing equities?

The satisfaction of legitimate human needs calls attention to the difficult problem of striking the right balance between population and resources. It also calls for recognition of the need to strike the right balance between protection for domestic agriculture (in such countries, for example, as Japan or France) and cheaper rice for the Japanese or cheaper wheat for the French. Moreover, in protecting legitimate human needs, the nations of the affluent triad—the United States, Japan, the European Community—must act to help relieve the great burden of debt that weighs so heavily on many developing countries. Often even affluent nations, such as the United States, must strike a balance between attending to important domestic problems and extending help to poor developing nations. The nature of that help is, of course, often a source of legitimate controversy. No one can assume that in the new world of international politics easy solutions to these problems will be found. But imaginative and prudent leaders can focus on the exploration of creative breakthroughs on each of these problems.

VI. THE PROMISE OF THE INFORMATION REVOLUTION

The information revolution holds out great hope for enhancing constitutional democracy around the globe, and for assisting governments to deal with economic, ecological, health, and other policy problems with greater speed and facility. Theoretically, this revolution can enhance constitutional democracy by making it difficult to conceal the brutality, ugliness, and degradation of war, political oppression, poverty, and ecological disasters. The information revolution, if it can avoid being captured by authoritarian regimes or self-seeking corporations, can make it increasingly difficult to ignore legitimate human needs. When problems of affordability, access, gatekeeping, and quality have been worked out, the information revolution can reinforce the rule of law, effective democratic governance, and prospects for freedom and prosperity. The success of the information revolution will depend upon respect for a democratic and constitutional culture. The interaction between such a culture and the information revolution should be a high priority not only of students of communication but also of students of the new world of international politics.

VII. CONCLUSION

The tragic war in the Persian Gulf in 1991 should not obscure the larger picture of a world in change. New thinking and developments—as they highlight creative breakthroughs in international politics—are highly encouraging. We are encouraged by certain creative political and economic breakthroughs that are moving us beyond the Cold War and the mortal danger of nuclear holocaust, beyond authoritarian regimes in Eastern Europe and elsewhere in the world, beyond a paralyzed or impotent United Nations, beyond narrow nationalistic economic policies, and beyond the abuse of science and new technology by authoritarian governments and selfish capitalistic interests. All of these breakthroughs, however, remain to be consolidated in the new world of international politics.

Moreover—and here we come realistically to the persistent dark side of international politics—we still struggle mightily to achieve breakthroughs to reduce significantly other patterns of violence in international politics, to break the grip of brutal and oppressive authoritarian regimes around the globe, and to overcome the gap between rich and poor peoples and nations in the world. The achievement of genuine security in the Middle East will remain a challenging problem after the end of the war in the Persian Gulf. However, the breakthroughs identified in the paragraph above, even if in need of consolidation, encourage us to look to the possibility of a creative breakthrough in the troubled Middle East.

The end of the Cold War, significant disarmament, the emergence of democratic and constitutional regimes in Eastern Europe, greater economic integration in all of Europe, and an invigorated United Nations will usher in a saner and sounder world, but not a utopia. Violent conflict will still be present and will demand the spread of democratic and constitutional operative ideals beyond the affluent developed nations. The consolidation of break-throughs to a new world of international politics will call for the emergence of a democratic and constitutional global ethos that will build on the repudiation of nuclear war in the West, on the commitment to political freedom, on the values of economic integration, freer trade, and globalization. The payoff of a peaceful and prosperous world will in time impress itself on all nations. Properly employed, the information revolution can assist in establishing the sense of this ethos.

The decade of the 1990s clearly holds out the promise of a 20th century ending without another world war. It also holds out the promise of a 21st century characterized by a free and prosperous Europe, North America, and Japan. However, it remains to be seen whether the Soviet Union can achieve the democratic and humane socialism to which Gorbachev seemingly aspires, or whether China will even opt for such a socialism. The plight of the Third World remains grim, but the prospect of peace among the superpowers holds out promise for a concerted effort to assist developing nations in significantly improving their lot in the 21st century. The achievement of patterns of peaceful coexistence in the Middle East may prove difficult, but it cannot be more difficult than the achievement of the end of the Cold war. Efforts in these endeavors will not be easy, and promises no easy successes. Nonetheless, there is hope for the peoples of the developing world. This hope, however, is contingent on a number of crucial "ifs." *If* the political and economic of the triad (United States, Europe, and Japan) can be maintained. *If* the Soviet Union and China also pursues the path of peace and economic well-being. *If* the United Nations can achieve patterns of collective security in the Middle East and in other troubled areas of the globe. *If* population and debt problems can be successfully addressed. *If* disarmament can move forward not only among the great powers but among all nations, great and small. *If* fanaticism and violence can be replaced by constitutional dialogue and peaceful change. Significant breakthroughs have occurred and are shaping a new world of international politics. Whether these breakthroughs will be consolidated still remains to be seen. What we now know, however, is that we can break through on problems that we once thought were not capable of solution. Buoyed by this knowledge, we can in the new world of international politics seek boldly, but prudently, to shape the emerging constitutional global order.

APPENDIXES

U.N. Security Council Resolution 661

Text of U.N. Resolution for
Sanctions on Iraq*

United Nations, August 6, 1990.

THE SECURITY COUNCIL,

Reaffirming its Resolution 660 (1990),

DEEPLY CONCERNED that this resolution has not been implemented and that the invasion by Iraq against Kuwait continues with further loss of human life and material destruction,
DETERMINED to bring the invasion and occupation of Kuwait by Iraq to an end and to restore the sovereignty, independence and territorial integrity of Kuwait,
NOTING that the legitimate government of Kuwait has expressed its readiness to comply with resolution 660 (1990),
MINDFUL of its responsibilities under the Charter for the maintenance of international peace and security,
AFFIRMING the inherent right of individual or collective self-defense, in response to the armed attack by Iraq against Kuwait, in accordance with Article 51 of the Charter,
ACTING under Chapter 7 of the Charter of the United Nations,

---

*See the *New York Times*, 7 August 1990, p. A9.

1.   **DETERMINES** that Iraq has failed to comply with operative paragraph 2 of Resolution 660 (1990) and has usurped the authority of the legitimate Government of Kuwait;

2.   **DECIDES,** as a consequence, to take the following measures to secure compliance of Iraq with operative paragraph 2 and to restore the authority of the legitimate Government of Kuwait;

3.   **DECIDES** that all states shall prevent:

a. The import into their territories of all commodities and products originating in Iraq or Kuwait exported therefrom after the date of this resolution;

b. Any activities by their nationals or in their territories which would promote or are calculated to promote the export or transshipment of any commodities or products from Iraq or Kuwait; and any dealings by their nationals or their flag vessels or in their territories in any commodities or products originating in Iraq or Kuwait and exported therefrom after the date of this resolution, including in particular any transfer of funds to Iraq or Kuwait for the purpose of such activities or dealings;

c. The sale or supply by their nationals or from their territories or using their flag vessels of any commodities or products, including weapons or any other military equipment, whether or not originating in their territories but not including supplies intended strictly for medical purposes, and, in humanitarian circumstances, foodstuffs, to any person or body in Iraq or Kuwait or to any person or body for the purposes of any business carried on in or operated from Iraq or Kuwait, and any activities by their nationals or in their territories which promote or are calculated to promote such sale, or supply or use of such commodities or products;

4.   **DECIDES** that all states shall not make available to the Government of Iraq or to any commercial, industrial or public utility undertaking in Iraq or Kuwait, any funds or any other financial or economic resources and shall prevent their nationals and any persons

within their territories from removing from their territories or otherwise making available to that government or any such undertaking any such funds or resources and from remitting any other funds to persons or bodies within Iraq or Kuwait, except payments exclusively for strictly medical or humanitarian purposes, and, in humanitarian circumstances, foodstuffs;

5.   **CALLS UPON** all states, including states nonmembers of the United Nations, to act strictly in accordance with the provisions of this resolution notwithstanding any contract entered into or license granted before the date of this resolution.

6.   **DECIDES** to establish, in accordance with Rule 28 of the provisional rules of procedure of the Security Council, a Committee of the Security Council consisting of all members of the Council, to undertake the following tasks and to report on its work to the Council with its observations and recommendations:

a. To examine the reports on the progress of the implementation of this resolution which will be submitted by the Secretary General;

b. To seek from all states further information regarding the action taken by them concerning the effective implementation of the provisions laid down in this resolution;

7.   **CALLS UPON** all states to cooperate fully with the Committee in the fulfillment of its task, including supplying such information as may be sought by the Committee in pursuance of this resolution;

8.   **REQUESTS** the Secretary General to provide all necessary assistance to the Committee and to make the necessary arrangements in the Secretariat for the purpose;

9.   **DECIDES** that, notwithstanding paragraphs 4 through 8, nothing in this resolution shall prohibit assistance to the legitimate Government of Kuwait, and **CALLS UPON** all states:

a. To take appropriate measures to protect assets of the legitimate government of Kuwait and its agencies; and

b. Not to recognize any regime set up by the occupying power;

10. **REQUESTS** the Secretary General to report to the Council on the progress of the implementation of this resolution, the first report to be submitted within 30 days;

11. **DECIDES** to keep this item on its agenda and to continue its efforts to put an early end to the invasion of Kuwait.

U.N. Security Council Resolution 678

Text of U.N. Resolution on
Using Force in the Gulf*

United Nations, November 29, 1990.

THE SECURITY COUNCIL,

RECALLING AND REAFFIRMING its Resolutions 660 (1990), 661 (1990), 662 (1990), 664 (1990), 665 (1990), 666 (1990), 667 (1990), 669 (1990), 670 (1990), 674 (1990), and 677 (1990),

NOTING that, despite all efforts by the United Nations, Iraq refuses to comply with its obligation to implement Resolution 660 (1990) and subsequent resolutions, in flagrant contempt of the Council,

MINDFUL of its duties and responsibilities under the Charter of the United Nations for the maintenance and preservation of international peace and security,

DETERMINED to secure full compliance with its decisions,

ACTING under Chapter VII of the Charter of the United Nations,

1.   **DEMANDS** that Iraq comply fully with Resolution 660 (1990) and all subsequent relevant resolutions and decides, while

---

*See the *New York Times*, November 1990.

maintaining all its decisions, to allow Iraq one final opportunity, as a pause of good will, to do so;

2.　**AUTHORIZES** member states cooperating with the Government of Kuwait, unless Iraq on or before Jan. 15, 1991, fully implements, as set forth in paragraph 1 above, the foregoing resolutions, to use all necessary means to uphold and implement the Security Council Resolution 660 and all subsequent relevant Resolutions and to restore international peace and security in the area;

3.　**REQUESTS** all states to provide appropriate support for the actions undertaken in pursuance of paragraph 2 of this resolution; and

4.　**REQUESTS** the states concerned to keep the Council regularly informed on the progress of actions undertaken pursuant to paragraphs 2 and 3 of this resolution;

5.　**DECIDES** to remain seized of this matter.